graphis annual '71/72

Editor: Walter Herdeg

Our society relies for its existence on the consumer behaviour of its members. And consumption depends on—inter alia—advertising.

Is this yearbook of advertising graphics, then, concerned with our society? Is it, indeed, a critical commentary on society? We leave the reader to form his own opinion.

Perhaps it will be an "committed" opinion; the verdict of the man who quite simply has to live in our times and in our society; who realizes that advertising —the communication of advertising concepts—exerts a greater influence than ever before on the shaping of our current environment.

Perhaps it may be that people in advertising—art directors, graphic designers, film and television people, consultants and even copywriters—will form opinions too. People who quite simply allow the book's many hundreds of examples of international advertising graphics to act upon them as a catalyst.

For the twentieth year, Walter Herdeg has now made his selection—from 19 780 works submitted—for *the* yearbook of international advertising. It provides a comprehensive survey of the newest, most striking examples of visual communication in advertising.

Its 240 pages, introduced in a foreword by a leading American graphic artist, Paul Rand, comprise 939 illustrations—169 of them in colour—with informative captions in English, German and French.

The book is divided into six chapters with 20 subject groups. An index simplifies the finding of particular works anywhere in this impressive and comprehensive anthology which has become an indispensable tool for everyone engaged in the field of visual communication.

Related Books for Graphic Designers

PHOTOGRAPHIS 71
Edited by Walter Herdeg

Here is volume six of the only international review devoted exclusively to outstanding achievements in advertising photography. Six sections, from the advertisement, booklet and poster to calendars, packaging and film and TV pictures, give a survey of the whole field. Introduction by Allan Porter, editor of *Camera*, Lucerne. Captions in three languages, personal and subject indexes, increase the practical value of this informative and stimulating work. 261 pages, 9½″ × 12″, 951 illustrations, 84 pages in colour.
$ 23.50

GRAPHIS / PACKAGING 2
Edited by Walter Herdeg

This second GRAPHIS volume on packaging, has been compiled in response to numerous requests. It takes into account the massive changes in packaging over the past decade. Over 1000 illustrations (accompanied by captions in three languages) present a cross-section of the best work being done today. The illustrations are grouped under eleven categories, ranging from food products to industrial containers, from pharmaceuticals to cosmetics. Preceding the various categories are introductory texts written be experts. A section on experimental work, and thorough indexes, complete a work which will be of inestimable value to all who work in the packaging field. 343 pages (74 in colour), 9½″ × 12″, 1111 illustrations, indexes.
$ 23.50

FILM & TV GRAPHICS
Edited by Walter Herdeg, Text by John Halas

"A beautiful and inspiring book, the graphics go far beyond the cel animation of the Disney era, and indicate a new integrated art of graphics, plus filmic development."—*Art Direction*. "These outstanding examples, originally conceived for movies and TV shows, offer an extraordinary wealth of pictorial invention in a wide diversity of personal styles, methods and media, an expert appraisal of the visual revolution initiated by the combination of graphic design and film."—*Film News*.
200 pages, 9½″ × 12″, 1079 illustrations, 122 in colour.
$16.50

Write for a complete catalogue:

VISUAL COMMUNICATION BOOKS

Hastings House, Publishers, 10 East 40th Street, New York, N.Y. 10016

graphis annual 1971/72

71|72 graphis annual

International Annual of Advertising Graphics

Internationales Jahrbuch der Werbegraphik

Art publicitaire graphique international

Edited by: / Herausgegeben von: / Réalisé par:

Walter Herdeg

Walter Herdeg, The Graphis Press, Zurich

Distributed in the United States by

Hastings House, Publishers, Inc.

10 EAST 40TH STREET, NEW YORK, N.Y. 10016

PUBLICATION N⁰ 123   (ISBN 8038-2648-6)

COPYRIGHT UNDER UNIVERSAL COPYRIGHT CONVENTION ©
COPYRIGHT 1971 BY WALTER HERDEG, THE GRAPHIS PRESS, 45 NUSCHELERSTRASSE, 8001 ZURICH, SWITZERLAND
PAPER/PAPIER: BIBER-KUNSTDRUCK SK 3 ADMIRO HOCHWEISS, 120 GM² UND WERKDRUCKPAPIER SK 3 BIBER-OFFSET
HOCHWEISS MASCHINENGLATT, 140 GM²
GEDRUCKT MIT FARBEN DER COLORA-GRAPHIKA AG, BERN / PRINTED WITH INKS OF COLORA-GRAPHIKA SA, BERNE
PRINTED IN SWITZERLAND

Contents

Inhalt

Sommaire

Abbreviations

Abkürzungen

Abréviations

PAUL RAND, now in his fifties, ranks among the great masters of graphic design in the twentieth century. He has practised advertising art at the highest level for many years, has taught it at leading schools and written about it in books that are now classics. In the introduction to this twentieth issue he sets forth lucidly the situation of the designer today, the task that faces him and the criteria by which he must measure his achievement. In the seas of change through which we are ploughing, beset by the multiple pollution of our material and mental habitat and buffeted by the waves of 'future shock', Rand's findings are the nearest thing to a sheet-anchor the designer could hope to put his trust in.

PAUL RAND, heute aktiver Fünfziger, ist seit 1936 als erfolgreicher Werbegrafiker tätig und gilt als einer der grossen Meister der Gebrauchsgrafik des zwanzigsten Jahrhunderts. Er lehrte Gebrauchsgrafik an führenden Schulen und schrieb darüber in Büchern, die jetzt als klassisch gelten. In der Einführung zu dieser zwanzigsten Ausgabe beleuchtet er die heutige Lage des Grafikers, die Aufgaben, vor die er gestellt ist und die Kriterien, denen er seine Arbeit anpassen muss. In den Wogen des Wandels, die uns umfluten, bedrängt durch die Verschmutzung unserer materiellen und geistigen Umwelt und dem «Zukunftsschock» ausgesetzt, sind die Grundsätze Paul Rands so etwas wie der Rettungsanker des heutigen Grafikers.

PAUL RAND, qui a aujourd'hui passé la cinquantaine, est l'un des grands maîtres de l'art graphique du XXe siècle. Depuis de nombreuses années, il pratique un art publicitaire de grande classe, l'enseigne dans des écoles réputées et y a consacré des ouvrages devenus de véritables classiques. En préfaçant ce 20e volume, il trace un portrait lucide du designer d'aujourd'hui, des tâches qui l'attendent, de l'échelle de valeurs qui permet de juger ses réalisations. L'esquif du designer est aujourd'hui ballotté par tant de flots tumultueux introduisant le changement perpétuel, la pollution matérielle et mentale, le choc du futur, que les conceptions de Rand pourraient bien fournir une ancre de salut des plus bienvenues.

No less than 19,790 items were submitted for this issue of GRAPHIS ANNUAL, of which—to take an example—1427 were posters. The Editor, who examined every one of these items, is thus fully qualified to judge the huge amount of work put into their preparation and despatch by our contributors. His thanks for their co-operation are all the more sincere, and the regret with which many good items were finally put aside was all the keener. A selection on this scale naturally involves many parameters. Should one include fine work that can hardly be adequately reproduced? How much space should one give to passing fads and fashions? Our aim is, in brief, to make a choice which, ten years hence, will still stand critical scrutiny.

Nicht weniger als 19 790 Arbeiten wurden für diese Ausgabe eingesandt, davon z. B. 1427 Plakate. Der Herausgeber, der jede einzelne Vorlage prüfte, kann den erheblichen Einsatz für Vorbereitung und Zustellung vollauf würdigen. Sein Dank an die Einsender ist deshalb um so grösser, wie auch sein Bedauern darüber, dass viele gute Arbeiten nicht gezeigt werden konnten. Eine solche Auswahl stellt naturgemäss Probleme. Sollen z. B. überdurchschnittliche Arbeiten, auch wenn sie sich schlecht reproduzieren lassen, trotzdem gezeigt werden? Wieviel Raum ist kurzlebigen Moden einzuräumen? Unser Ziel ist, die Auswahl so zu treffen, dass sie auch in zehn Jahren einer kritischen Beurteilung noch standhalten wird.

Le présent volume représente le meilleur de 19 790 envois, dont 1427 affiches, etc. Après avoir examiné la totalité de ces productions, la Rédaction peut apprécier à sa juste mesure l'effort impressionnant de nos collaborateurs, ce qui lui fait d'autant plus regretter d'avoir dû écarter nombre de bons travaux. Que tous ceux qui ont bien voulu contribuer à ce panorama de l'art graphique trouvent ici nos remerciements les plus sincères. La sélection opérée implique un grand nombre de paramètres. Fallait-il retenir des travaux excellents en soi, mais difficiles à reproduire? Quelle place était-on en droit de faire aux modes passagères? Notre but a été, en bref, de présenter un choix qui pourra résister à la critique de la décennie à venir.

Introduction

We are told that 'One picture is worth more than ten thousand words', but is it? Does any one picture in this colourful collection of GRAPHIS ANNUAL tell us of the compromises, doubts, frustrations, misunderstandings, that go into making an ad, a poster, a trade mark, a book jacket, a letterhead, a TV commercial?

Some years ago I was asked to contribute a paper on the subject of the visual arts.[1] Those problems I chose to write about have, if anything, become even more apparent today than they were then. For the most part neither time, nostalgia, Victoriana, Art Deco, nor any other fashionable revival has warranted any substantial alterations in my views.

Courage and Creativity

Like that of the spawning salmon, the artist's life is a never-ending upstream battle. To function creatively the artist must have the courage to fight for what he believes. Courage in the face of a danger that has no element of high adventure in it—just the cold, hard possibility of losing his job. Yet the courage of his convictions is, along with his talent, his only source of strength. Frank Lloyd Wright put it this way:[2]

'I'll work as I'll think as I am
No thought of fashion or sham
Nor for fortune the jade
Serve vile Gods of trade
My thought as beseemeth a man'

The businessman will never respect the professional who does not believe in what he does. The businessman under these circumstances can only 'use' the artist for his own ends. And why not, if the artist himself has no ends?

In asking the artist to have courage, we must ask the same of industry. The impetus to conform, so widespread today, will, if not checked, kill all forms of creativity, scientific and technological included.

Business has a strong tendency to wait for a few brave pioneers to produce or underwrite original work, then rush to climb on the bandwagon. The bandwagon, of course, may not even be going in the right direction. The attention and admiration evoked by the high calibre of XYZ's advertising have induced many an advertiser to say 'Let's do something like XYZ' without considering that it might not be at all suited to his needs. Specific problems require specific visual solutions. But both XYZ's and ABC's advertising and products can be made to fulfil their functions and also be aesthetically gratifying. Both can express respect for and concern with the broadest interests of the consumer.

Against the outstanding achievements in design by some companies, there stands the great dismal mountain of lacklustre work. On the whole, industry lacks confidence in creative talent and creative work, and this is the most serious obstacle to raising the standards of design.

Artistic Integrity

There are those who believe that the role the designer must play is fixed and determined by the socio-economic climate; that he must discover his functional niche and fit himself into it. It seems to me that this ready-made image ignores the part the artist can play in creating this climate. Whether as advertising tycoons, missile builders, public or private citizens, we are all human beings, and to endure we must, first of all, be *for* ourselves. It is only when man is not accepted as the centre of human concern that it becomes feasible to create a system of production which values profit out of proportion to responsible public service, or to design ads in which the only aesthetic criteria are the use of fashionable illustrations and 'in' type faces.

The commercial artist (designer) who wants to be more than a mere stylist and who wishes to avoid being overwhelmed by the demands of clients, the idiosyncrasies of public taste, and the ambiguities of consumer research surveys must become clear as to what his cultural contribution should be. In all these areas he must try to distinguish the real from the imaginary, the sincere from the pretentious, and the objective from the biased.

If the commercial artist has both talent and a commitment to aesthetic values, he will automatically try to make the product of graphic design both pleasing and visually stimulating to the user or the viewer. By stimulating I mean that this work will add something to the spectator's experience.

The artist must believe his work is an aesthetic statement, but he must also understand his general role in society. It is this role that justifies his spending the client's money and his risking other people's jobs. And it entitles him to make mistakes. He adds something to the world. He gives it new ways of feeling and of thinking. He opens doors to new experience. He provides new alternatives as solutions to old problems.

There is nothing wrong with selling, even with 'hard' selling, but selling which misrepresents, condescends, relies on sheer gullibility or stupidity is wrong. Morally, it is very difficult for an artist to do a direct and creative job if dishonest claims are being made for the product he is asked to advertise, or if, as an industrial designer, he is supposed to exercise mere stylistic ingenuity to give an old product a new appearance. The artist's sense of worth depends on his feeling of integrity. If this is destroyed, he will no longer be able to function creatively.

Art and Communication

The lament of the graphic designer that he is not permitted to do good work because good work is neither wanted nor understood by his employers is universal. It is indeed very often true. But if the artist honestly evaluates his work he will frequently find that the 'good work' the businessman has rejected is really not so 'good'. Many times when the 'square' client says 'it's too far out', he may be unconsciously reacting to inappropriate symbolism, obscure interpretation of an idea, poor typography, an inadequate display of his product, or simply bad communication. In a new edition of my book THOUGHTS ON DESIGN,[3] this problem was alluded to as follows:

Graphic design—
which fulfils aesthetic needs,
complies with the laws of form
and the exigencies of two-dimensional space;
which speaks in semiotics, sans-serifs,
and geometrics;
which abstracts, transforms, translates,
rotates, dilates, repeats, mirrors,
groups, and regroups—
is not good design
if it is irrelevant.
Graphic design—
which evokes the symmetria of Vitruvius,
the dynamic symmetry of Hambidge,
the asymmetry of Mondrian;
which is a good gestalt;
which is generated by intuition or by computer,
by invention or by a system or coordinates—
is not good design
if it does not co-operate
as an instrument
in the service of communication.

Originality and Subject-Matter

Ideas do not need to be esoteric to be original or exciting. As H. L. Mencken says of Shaw's plays, 'The roots of each one of them are in platitude; the roots of *every* effective stage play are in platitude.' And when he asks why Shaw is able to 'kick up such a pother', he answers, 'For the simplest of reasons. Because he practises with great zest and skill the fine art of exhibiting the obvious in unexpected and terrifying lights.'[4] From Impressionism to Pop, the commonplace and the comic strip have become the ingredients for the artist's cauldron. What Cézanne did with apples, Picasso with guitars, Léger with machines, Schwitters with rubbish, and Duchamp with urinals makes it clear that revelation does not depend upon grandiose concepts. In 1947 I wrote what I still hold to be true, 'The problem of the artist is to make the commonplace uncommonplace.'[5]

If artistic quality depended on exalted subject-matter, the commercial artist, as well as the advertising agency and advertiser, would be in a bad way. For years I have worked with light bulb manufacturers, cigar makers, distillers, etc., whose products visually are not in themselves unusual. A light bulb is almost as commonplace as an apple, but if I fail to make a package or an advertisement for light bulbs that is lively and original, it will not be the light bulb that is at fault.

The 'Corporate Image'

In this, the speed generation, practically any corporation, large or small, can have its 'image' made to order. A vast army of image makers have made a business out of art large enough almost to rival the businesses they help to portray.

Much has been touted about the virtues of corporate identification programmes. Because the corporate image so often conveys the impression that it is all-encompassing, it leaves little doubt in the mind of the onlooker that the image he sees represents a company which is really in the swim, that it's the best, the first, and the most. However, being *with it* is not always being *for it*.

It seems to me that a company can more easily be recognized for what it really believes not by its 'made to order image' (its trade mark, logotype, letterhead), nor by the number of avant-garde prints or Mies van der Rohe chairs which embellish its offices, but by its more mundane, day-to-day activities: its house organs, counter displays, trade advertisements, packaging and products. Unless it consistently represents the aims and beliefs as well as the total production and activities of a company, a corporate image is at best mere window dressing, and at worst deception.

Things can be made and marketed without our considering their moral or aesthetic aspects; ads can convince without pleasing or heightening the spectator's visual awareness, products can work regardless of their appearance. But should they? The world of business could function without benefit of art—but should it? I think not, if only for the simple reason that the world would be a poorer place if it did.

PAUL RAND

References:

[1] Daedalus, Winter 1960, in collaboration with Ann Rand.
[2] Frank Lloyd Wright, WORK SONG, Oak Park Workshop, 1896.
[3] Paul Rand, THOUGHTS ON DESIGN (Studio Vista, London, 1970; Van Nostrand Reinhold, USA, and Zokeisha, Japan, 1971), p. 9.
[4] H. L. Mencken, PREJUDICES: A SELECTION (New York: Vintage K 58, Alfred A. Knopf, 1958), pp. 27 and 28.
[5] Paul Rand, THOUGHTS ON DESIGN (New York: George Wittenborn, Inc., 1947), p. 53.

Vorwort

Es heisst, «ein Bild sagt mehr als zehntausend Worte» – aber stimmt das auch? Erzählt uns ein einziges Bild dieser farbigen Sammlung in Graphis Annual von den Kompromissen, Zweifeln, Frustrationen und Missverständnissen, die bei der Entstehung einer Anzeige, eines Plakates, eines Warenzeichens, eines Buchumschlages, eines Briefkopfes oder eines Werbefilms im Spiele sind?

Vor einigen Jahren hat man mich um einen Beitrag zum Thema «bildende Künste»[1] gebeten. Die Probleme, über die ich mich damals zu schreiben entschloss, sind heute vielleicht noch offenkundiger geworden als damals. Im grossen und ganzen haben weder Zeitablauf, sentimentale Sehnsucht nach den guten alten Zeiten, Jugendstil noch irgendeine andere modische Wiederbelebung eine wesentliche Änderung meiner Auffassungen notwendig gemacht.

Mut und Kreativität

Wie der Lachs während der Laichzeit, so muss der Künstler sein ganzes Leben lang gegen den Strom ankämpfen. Um schöpferisch tätig zu sein, muss der Künstler den Mut haben, für das zu kämpfen, woran er glaubt. Mut im Angesicht einer Gefahr, die nichts grossartig Abenteuerliches an sich hat – nur die kalte, harte Möglichkeit, seinen Job zu verlieren. Doch das Handeln gemäss der eigenen Überzeugung ist, zusammen mit seiner Begabung, seine einzige Quelle der Kraft. Frank Lloyd Wright[2] hat das etwa so ausgedrückt:

«Ich will schaffen, wie ich glaube zu sein
Ohne Gedanken an Mode und Schein
Nicht für Reichtum und buhlerisch Glück
Opf're ich niedrigem Händlergeschick
Meinen Geist – so soll's bei einem Manne sein.»

Der Geschäftsmann wird niemals den Berufskünstler respektieren, der nicht an das glaubt, was er tut. Sonst könnte er den Künstler nur für seine eigenen Ziele «benutzen». Und warum nicht, wenn der Künstler selbst keine Ziele hat?

Wenn wir vom Künstler Mut fordern, müssen wir dasselbe auch von der Industrie verlangen. Der heute so mächtige Drang zur Konformität wird, wenn man ihm nicht Einhalt gebietet, alle Spielarten der Kreativität abtöten, einschliesslich der wissenschaftlichen und technologischen.

Im Geschäftsleben besteht die starke Tendenz, auf ein paar wackere Pioniere zu warten, die originelle Arbeiten produzieren oder fördern, um sich dann eiligst dem erfolgversprechenden Kurs anzuschliessen. Ob dieser Kurs aber auch in jedem Falle Erfolg hat, ist natürlich noch lange nicht sicher. Die dem hohen Format der Werbung von XYZ gezollte Aufmerksamkeit und Bewunderung haben schon manchen Inserenten veranlasst zu sagen: «Lasst uns doch etwas Ähnliches wie XYZ unternehmen», ohne dabei zu überlegen, dass dies vielleicht überhaupt nicht seinen Bedürfnissen entspricht. Verschiedene Probleme müssen mit verschiedenen Mitteln sichtbar gemacht werden. Aber sowohl XYZ's wie auch ABC's Werbung und Produkte können so gestaltet werden, dass sie ihre Funktionen erfüllen und ausserdem ästhetisch befriedigen. Beide können Rücksicht und Bezugnahme auf die breitesten Interessen des Verbrauchers ausdrücken.

Gegen die hervorragenden Leistungen einiger Gesellschaften in künstlerischer Gestaltung aber hebt sich der grosse, trostlose Berg der glanz- und farblosen Arbeiten ab. Im grossen und ganzen fehlt der Industrie das Vertrauen in kreative Arbeit und kreatives Talent, und dies ist das bedeutendste Hindernis auf dem Wege zur Hebung der Qualität künstlerischen Gestaltens.

Künstlerische Integrität

Manche Leute glauben, dass die Rolle, die der Designer spielen muss, von dem sozialen und wirtschaftlichen Klima der Gesellschaft geprägt und ausgerichtet wird; dass er seinen ihm zukommenden Platz aufspüren und sich dementsprechend anpassen muss. Mir scheint, dass diese konventionelle Vorstellung den Anteil des Künstlers ignoriert, den dieser selbst bei der Schaffung dieses Klimas ausüben kann. Ob nun als Werbemagnat, Fernlenkraketenbauer, Beamter oder einfacher Bürger, wir sind alle nur Menschen, und um als solche zu überleben, müssen wir in erster Linie für uns selbst dasein. Nur wenn der Mensch nicht als Mittelpunkt des menschlichen Interesses akzeptiert wird, ist es möglich, ein Produktionssystem zu schaffen, das den Profit in gar keinem Verhältnis zur Verantwortung gegenüber dem Dienst an der Öffentlichkeit bewertet, oder Anzeigen zu gestalten, deren einziges ästhetisches Kriterium die Verwendung von modischen Illustrationen und Schriftarten ist, die gerade «in» sind.

Der graphische Gestalter oder Designer, der mehr als nur modischer Stilist sein und nicht von den Forderungen der Klienten, den Idiosynkrasien des Publikumsgeschmacks und den vieldeutigen Konsumforschungsberichten überwältigt werden möchte, muss sich darüber klar werden, wie sein eigener kultureller Beitrag aussehen soll. Auf all diesen Gebieten muss er versuchen, das Echte von dem Unechten, das Schlichte von dem Prätentiösen und das Objektive von dem Voreingenommenen zu unterscheiden.

Wenn der Gestalter Talent besitzt und sich den ästhetischen Wertbegriffen verpflichtet fühlt, wird er automatisch versuchen, das Produkt graphischer Gestaltung für den Benutzer oder Betrachter sowohl gefällig als auch optisch anregend zu machen. Mit anregend meine ich, dass seine Arbeit in irgendeiner Weise das Wissen oder die Kenntnisse des Betrachters bereichert.

Der Künstler muss daran glauben, dass seine Arbeit eine ästhetische Aussage ist, aber er muss auch seine generelle Rolle in der Gesellschaft verstehen. Denn diese Rolle ist es, die ihn rechtfertigt, das Geld seiner Klienten auszugeben und anderer Leute Arbeitsplätze aufs Spiel zu setzen. Und sie berechtigt ihn dazu, Fehler zu machen. Er gibt der Welt etwas. Er zeigt ihr neue Wege des Fühlens und Denkens. Er öffnet Tore zu neuen Erkenntnissen. Er bietet neue Alternativen als Lösungen für alte Probleme.

Gegen Reklame, selbst gegen «harte» Reklame, ist nichts einzuwenden, es sei denn, dass sie etwas vortäuscht, kein Niveau hat und sich nur auf Leichtgläubigkeit oder Dummheit verlässt. Vom moralischen Standpunkt aus ist es sehr schwer für einen Graphiker, eine ehrliche und kreative Arbeit zu schaffen, wenn betrügerische Ansprüche für das Produkt erhoben werden, das er anpreisen soll, oder wenn er als Produktgestalter lediglich seinen Einfallsreichtum aufbieten soll, um einem alten Produkt durch modische Mätzchen den Anschein des Neuen zu geben. Das Gespür des Künstlers für inneren Wert hängt von seinem Gefühl für Integrität ab. Wenn dieses zerstört ist, wird er nicht länger kreativ tätig sein können.

Kunst und Kommunikation

Die Klage des Graphikers, dass man ihm nicht gestattet, gute Arbeit zu liefern, weil gute Arbeit von seinen Auftraggebern weder gewünscht noch verstanden wird, ist weltumspannend. Und sie beruht in der Tat sehr oft auf Wahrheit. Doch wenn der Graphiker sein Werk ehrlich bewertet, wird er häufig erkennen, dass seine vom Geschäftsmann zurückgewiesene «gute Arbeit» in Wirklichkeit gar nicht so «gut» ist. Sehr oft, wenn der «spiessbürgerliche» Klient hartnäckig behauptet, die Sache sei «zu weit hergeholt», mag er unbewusst auf eine unpassende Symbolik, die unverständliche Interpretation einer Idee, unzureichende Hervorhebung seines Produktes oder einfach schlechte Kommunikation reagieren. In einer Neuauflage meines Buches «THOUGHTS ON DESIGN»[3] habe ich dieses Problem folgendermassen angesprochen:

Graphische Gestaltung –
die ästhetische Ansprüche erfüllt,
den Gesetzen der Form entspricht
und den Erfordernissen des zweidimensionalen Raums;
die sich in Symbolen, Groteskbuchstaben
und geometrischen Proportionen ausdrückt;
die abstrahiert, transformiert, umsetzt,
auswechselt, ausweitet, wiederholt, spiegelt,
gruppiert und neugruppiert –
ist keine gute graphische Gestaltung,
wenn sie nicht sachbezüglich ist.
Graphische Gestaltung –
die die Ausgewogenheit eines Vitruvius beschwört,
die dynamische Symmetrie eines Hambidge,
die Asymmetrie eines Mondrian;
die eine «gute Gestalt» aufweist;
die von Eingebung oder von einem Computer
hervorgebracht wurde,
durch Einfallsreichtum oder ein System von Koordinaten –
ist keine gute graphische Gestaltung,
wenn sie nicht ihren Beitrag leistet
als ein Instrument
im Dienste der Kommunikation.

Originalität und Thema

Ideen müssen nicht esoterisch sein, um originell oder erregend zu sein. So sagt beispielsweise H. L. Mencken von

Shaws Stücken: «Ein jedes von ihnen wurzelt in der Platitüde; die Wurzeln eines *jeden* wirkungsvollen Bühnenwerks erwachsen aus der Platitüde.» Und wenn er fragt, warum Shaw denn soviel «Staub aufwirbeln» kann, antwortet er, «Aus dem allereinfachsten Grunde. Weil er nämlich mit viel Würze und grossem Geschick die feine Kunst praktiziert, das Offenkundige in ein unerwartetes oder erschreckendes Licht zu setzen.»[4] Vom Impressionismus bis zum Pop sind Gemeinplatz und Comic Strip die Gewürze im Hexenkessel des Künstlers. Was Cézanne mit Äpfeln, Picasso mit Gitarren, Léger mit Maschinen, Schwitters mit Abfall und Duchamp mit Nachttöpfen erreichte, macht klar, dass etwas Grossartiges nicht von grossartigen Themen abhängt. Schon 1947 schrieb ich, was ich immer noch für richtig halte: «Das Problem des Künstlers ist es, das Gewöhnliche ungewöhnlich erscheinen zu lassen!»[5]

Das Erscheinungsbild (Corporate Image)

In dieser schnellebigen, erfolgsbetonten Generation kann praktisch jede Gesellschaft ihr «Image» auf Bestellung haben. Ein zahlloses Heer von Image-Machern hat aus dieser Kunst ein fast so grosses Geschäft gemacht wie die Unternehmen, deren Bild sie zu gestalten helfen.

Die Vorzüge der sogenannten *Corporate Identification Programmes* sind über den grünen Klee gelobt worden. Weil nämlich das Erscheinungsbild so oft den Eindruck vermittelt, dass es allumfassend ist, lässt es den Betrachter kaum daran zweifeln, dass das Bild, das er sieht, eine Gesellschaft repräsentiert, die wirklich auf dem laufenden, die die beste, die erste und die grösste ist. In Wirklichkeit bedeutet Mitmachen nicht immer auch Dafürsein.

Mir scheint, dass man das, wovon ein Unternehmen ehrlich überzeugt ist, nicht so einfach an seinem «auf Bestellung gelieferten Firmenstil» (Warenzeichen, Logotype, Briefkopf), an der Zahl der avantgardistischen Lithographien oder Mies-van-der-Rohe-Stühle in seinen Büroräumen erkennen kann, sondern viel eher an seiner mehr weltlich ausgerichteten, sich täglich wiederholenden Tätigkeit: an seiner Hauszeitschrift, Warenauslage, seinen Verkaufsanzeigen, Verpackungen und Produkten. Wenn das Erscheinungsbild nicht übereinstimmend die Ziele und Überzeugungen wie auch die gesamte Produktion und Tätigkeit eines Unternehmens repräsentiert, ist es bestenfalls Schönfärberei, schlimmstenfalls jedoch Betrug.

Waren können hergestellt und auf den Markt geworfen werden, ohne dass wir ihre moralischen oder ästhetischen Aspekte abwägen; Anzeigen können überzeugen, ohne das Vorstellungsvermögen des Betrachters zu bereichern oder ihm zu gefallen, Produkte können ohne Rücksicht auf ihr Aussehen ihren Zweck erfüllen. Aber sollten sie das? Die Geschäftswelt könnte auch ohne die Mithilfe der Kunst funktionieren – aber sollte sie das? Ich glaube nicht, und sei es auch nur aus dem einfachen Grunde, dass die Welt dann um vieles ärmer wäre.

Hinweise: siehe Seite 13.

PAUL RAND

Préface

On dit communément qu'«une seule image vaut plus de dix mille mots», mais est-ce vrai? Y a-t-il dans cette collection de GRAPHIS ANNUAL si variée et haute en couleur une seule image qui nous parle des compromis, des doutes, des frustrations, des malentendus qui ont accompagné la création d'une annonce, d'une affiche, d'une marque, d'une jaquette de livre, d'un en-tête, d'un film publicitaire pour la télé?

Il y a quelques années, on me sollicita d'écrire un article sur les arts visuels.[1] Les problèmes que j'y discutai sont aujourd'hui encore bien plus visibles qu'alors. Dans l'ensemble, ni le temps, ni la nostalgie, ni les modes du victorianisme ou de l'art nouveau ou une autre forme de retour en arrière comme on les aime à notre époque n'ont influencé substantiellement mes opinions.

Courage et Créativité

Tout comme le jeune saumon à l'époque du frai, l'artiste est engagé toute sa vie durant dans une lutte à contre-courant. Afin de pouvoir fournir une œuvre vraiment créative, l'artiste doit avoir le courage de lutter pour ses convictions. Du courage face à un danger qui ne comporte aucun élément d'exaltation – juste la froide et dure possibilité de perdre son job. Et pourtant, le courage qu'il emploie à lutter pour ses convictions est, avec ses ressources de talent, la seule source où l'artiste peut puiser de l'énergie. C'est ce que Frank Lloyd Wright exprima jadis en ces mots:[2]

«*Je travaillerai comme je penserai, comme je suis,*
Sans songer à la mode ou à l'artifice mensonger,
Ni pour la fortune, cette femme légère,
Ne servirai les vils dieux du commerce.
Je réaliserai ma pensée, comme il sied à un homme.»

L'homme d'affaires ne respectera jamais le professionnel qui ne croit pas à ce qu'il fait. Dans de telles circonstances, l'homme d'affaires ne peut qu'«utiliser» l'artiste à ses propres fins. Et pourquoi pas, si l'artiste ne poursuit pas de but à lui?

Si nous demandons à l'artiste d'être courageux, il faut aussi demander ce courage à l'industrie. Le réflexe si général de conformisme risque, si on n'y fait échec, de paralyser à la longue toutes les formes de créativité, y compris ses aspects scientifiques et technologiques.

Dans le monde des affaires, on a une forte tendance à attendre patiemment que quelques pionniers audacieux produisent ou souscrivent le risque d'un travail original pour ensuite se précipiter aux côtés du téméraire à qui la fortune sourit, même s'il s'est engagé dans une voie fausse. L'intérêt et l'admiration que remporte la création publicitaire très originale de XYZ fait que plus d'un annonceur se sent tenté de faire «quelque chose dans le genre de XYZ», sans tenir compte du fait que cette publicité ne vaut peut-être pas grand-chose pour ses besoins fort différents de ceux du client d'XYZ. A problème spécifique, solution visuelle spécifique. Les deux manières publicitaires, celle de XYZ et celle de ABC, ainsi que les produits qu'elles mettent en relief peuvent être conçus de façon optimale et esthétiquement satisfaisante à la fois. Les deux peuvent être également aptes à exprimer le respect dû au consommateur et le souci de ses intérêts essentiels.

Face aux réalisations hors pair, dans le domaine du design, de quelques sociétés se dresse dans une morne plaine le triste terril des productions sans lustre. En général, l'industrie n'a guère confiance dans le talent créateur et le travail créateur, et ce manque de confiance constitue l'obstacle majeur à l'élévation du niveau du design.

Intégrité artistique

Il y en a qui pensent que le rôle que le designer est appelé à jouer est déterminé et fixé par le climat socio-économique où il se meut; que ce qu'il a à faire, c'est découvrir sa niche fonctionnelle et s'adapter à l'espace vacant. Il me semble que cette image toute faite néglige la part qui peut revenir à l'artiste dans l'élaboration dudit climat. Que nous soyons de grosses huiles en publicité, des constructeurs de missiles, d'humbles citoyens ou des personnalités publiques, nous sommes tous des êtres humains; pour durer, nous devons avant tout être là *pour* nous-mêmes. C'est seulement lorsque l'homme n'est pas accepté comme centre des préoccupations humaines qu'il devient possible d'ériger un système de production où le profit prend une importance démesurée par rapport à l'intérêt public, ou de concevoir une publicité dont les seuls critères esthétiques sont l'emploi d'illustrations en vogue et d'une typographie dans le vent.

L'artiste publicitaire (le designer) qui entend être plus qu'un simple styliste et qui veut éviter d'être accablé par les exigences de la clientèle, les impondérables du goût public et les résultats ambigus des sondages d'opinion doit s'interroger avec toute la clarté possible sur sa contribution culturelle. Dans tous ces domaines, il doit essayer de distinguer le réel de l'imaginaire, le sincère du prétentieux, l'objectif du partisan.

Si l'artiste publicitaire a du talent en même temps qu'un idéal esthétique affirmé, il essaiera automatiquement de rendre le produit de sa création graphique à la fois attrayant et visuellement efficace pour la stimulation de l'usager ou de l'acheteur potentiel. Par stimulation, j'entends enrichissement de l'expérience du consommateur.

L'artiste doit être persuadé que son travail est un message esthétique, mais il doit aussi être conscient de son rôle général au sein de la société. C'est ce rôle qui justifie la dépense qu'il fait de l'argent du client et les risques qu'il fait courir aux emplois d'autrui. Ce rôle l'autorise aussi à commettre des erreurs. Il ajoute quelque chose au monde. Il crée de nouvelles possibilités d'expériences émotionnelles et intellectuelles. Il offre des alternatives nouvelles à la solution de problèmes anciens.

Il n'y a rien à reprocher à la vente, même à la vente acharnée. Mais la vente qui dénature les faits, qui se fait condescendante, qui table sur la crédulité des acheteurs ou leur niaiserie, cette vente-là s'engage sur une voie fausse. Moralement, il est très difficile pour un artiste de faire œuvre valable et créatrice si le produit est présenté sous un jour fallacieux ou si on lui demande en tant qu'esthéticien industriel de se borner à habiller de neuf un produit ancien. Le sens aigu que peut avoir un artiste de la valeur de sa création est tributaire de son sentiment d'intégrité. Si sa conviction de faire œuvre intègre est détruite, on lui enlève la possibilité de fonctionner de manière créatrice.

Art et Communication

C'est un phénomène universel que l'artiste graphique se plaigne de ne pouvoir faire du bon travail parce que le bon travail n'est ni désiré ni compris par ses clients et employeurs. Cette plainte n'est souvent que trop justifiée. Toutefois, si l'artiste apprécie son travail à sa juste valeur, honnêtement, il découvrira que le «bon travail» refusé par l'homme d'affaires n'est pas toujours aussi «bon» qu'il le croyait. Très souvent, le client qui tranche en lançant: «c'est hors du sujet» peut fort bien réagir inconsciemment à un symbolisme impropre, une interprétation obscure d'une idée, une piteuse typographie, une mise en valeur inadéquate de son produit, ou tout simplement un manque de communicabilité. J'ai fait mention de ce problème dans la nouvelle édition de mon livre THOUGHTS ON DESIGN (Réflexions sur le Design)[3], en disant que:

Le design graphique –
qui satisfait à des besoins esthétiques,
se conforme aux lois de la forme
et aux exigences de l'espace bidimensionnel;
qui s'exprime en termes séméiologiques, en sans sérif
et en notions géométriques;
qui abstrait, transforme, transpose,
opère des rotations, dilatations, répétitions, réflexions,
groupe et regroupe –
n'est pas du bon design
s'il est hors de propos.
Le design graphique –
qui évoque la symétrie de Vitruve,
la symétrie dynamique de Hambidge,
l'asymétrie de Mondrian;
qui produit une bonne gestalt;
qui est engendré par l'intuition ou l'ordinateur,
par l'invention ou un système de coordonnées –
n'est pas du bon design
s'il ne coopère pas
en tant qu'instrument
au service de la communication.

Originalité et Sujet

Une idée n'a pas besoin d'être ésotérique pour être originale ou stimulante. Comme le dit H. L. Mencken des pièces de Shaw, «les racines de chacune d'elles plongent dans l'insipide; les racines de *toute* pièce réussie plongent dans l'insipide.» Et lorsqu'il se demande pourquoi Shaw est capable de faire si grand bruit à partir de rien, il fournit la réponse suivante: «pour la plus simple des raisons. Parce qu'il exerce avec mordant et une habileté consommée l'art achevé de présenter l'évident dans un jour inattendu et terrifiant.»[4] De l'impressionnisme au pop, le lieu commun

et la bande dessinée sont devenus des ingrédients permanents dans le chaudron de l'artiste. Ce que Cézanne a fait des pommes, Picasso des guitares, Léger des machines, Schwitters des détritus, Duchamp des urinaux démontre clairement que la révélation ne dépend pas de conceptions grandioses. En 1947, j'écrivais ce que je pense toujours être vrai, à savoir que «le problème de l'artiste est de débanaliser le banal.»[5]

Si la qualité en art dépendait d'un sujet ou thème exalté, l'artiste publicitaire, tout comme l'agence de publicité et l'annonceur, seraient en bien piteux état. Depuis des années, je travaille avec des fabricants d'ampoules électriques, de cigares, des distillateurs, etc., dont les produits n'ont rien de sensationnel, visuellement parlé. Une ampoule est chose aussi courante et banale qu'une pomme, mais si je ne réussis pas à créer un emballage ou une annonce pour cette ampoule qui soient originaux et vivants, ce ne sera pas de la faute de l'ampoule.

L'Image globale d'entreprise

Dans notre génération éprise de vitesse, n'importe quel groupe de sociétés, grand ou petit, peut se faire préparer une «image globale» faite sur mesure. Une légion de faiseurs d'image ont converti leur art en une affaire presque aussi importante que celles dont ils établissent le portrait.

On a clamé à cor et à cri les vertus des programmes d'identification globale d'une entreprise. Comme l'image globale de marque fait souvent l'impression de saisir l'intégrale réalité, elle convainc sans peine l'observateur que l'image qu'on lui montre représente une société qui a le vent dans les voiles, est la meilleure, la première, le nec plus ultra. Toutefois, il est utile de se rappeler que ce qui est présent à notre esprit n'emporte pas forcément toujours la conviction.

Il me semble qu'une société est plus aisément reconnaissable par ses convictions réelles: non pas par son image de marque toute faite (marque de fabrique, logotype, entête), ni par le nombre d'estampes d'avant-garde ou de fauteuils signés Mies van der Rohe qui ornent ses bureaux, mais par ses activités plus terre à terre, plus proches de la réalité quotidienne: ses publications internes, ses éléments publicitaires pour points de vente, ses annonces professionnelles, ses emballages et ses produits. A moins de coller à la réalité des buts et convictions d'une société, à la totalité de sa production et de ses activités, une image globale de marque est au mieux de la simple décoration d'étalage, au pire de la supercherie pure et simple.

Des produits peuvent se fabriquer et se distribuer sans que nous ayons à considérer leurs aspects moraux ou esthétiques; une annonce peut convaincre sans séduire ou enrichir la réceptibilité visuelle du lecteur; des produits peuvent donner satisfaction et ne pas payer de mine. Mais le devraient-ils? Le monde des affaires pourrait fonctionner sans se parer des avantages de l'art – mais le devrait-il? Je pense que non, et ne serait-ce que pour la simple raison que la terre serait un endroit bien désolé si tel était le cas.

Bibliographie: voir page 13.

PAUL RAND

Hinweise:

[1] Daedalus, Winter 1960, in Zusammenarbeit mit Ann Rand.
[2] Frank Lloyd Wright, WORK SONG, Oak Park Workshop, 1896.
[3] Paul Rand, THOUGHTS ON DESIGN (Studio Vista, London 1970; Van Nostrand Reinhold, USA, und Zokeisha, Japan, 1971), Seite 9.
[4] H.L.Mencken, PREJUDICES: A SELECTION (New York: Vintage K 58, Alfred A.Knopf, 1958), Seiten 27 und 28.
[5] Paul Rand, THOUGHTS ON DESIGN (New York: George Wittenborn, Inc., 1947), Seite 53.

Bibliographie:

[1] Daedalus, Hiver 1960, en collaboration avec Ann Rand.
[2] Frank Lloyd Wright, WORK SONG, Oak Park Workshop, 1896.
[3] Paul Rand, THOUGHTS ON DESIGN (Studio Vista, Londres, 1970; Van Nostrand Reinhold, USA, et Zokeisha, Japon, 1971), p. 9.
[4] H.L.Mencken, PREJUDICES: A SELECTION (New York, Vintage K 58, Alfred A.Knopf, 1958), pp. 27 et 28.
[5] Paul Rand, THOUGHTS ON DESIGN (New York: George Wittenborn, Inc., 1947), p. 53.

Index to Designers and Artists
Verzeichnis der Entwerfer und Künstler
Index des maquettistes et artistes

GUHL, LOUIS; Zürich. 623
GUIDOTTI, PAOLO; Milan. 690
GUIRÉ-VAKA, MICHEL; Paris. 271, 272, 332–334,
   338, 339, 341–343

HAARS, PETER; Lillestrøm/NOR. 117
HACHIMURA, KUNIO; Tokyo. 807
HAINES, WILLIAM & CURRIE; Los Angeles. 560
HALL, STEPHEN; San Francisco. 448
HALLOCK, ROBERT; Newtown/USA. 634
HALMEN, PET; Düsseldorf. 138
HAMPTON, BLAKE; Weston, Conn. 257
HANE, ROGER; New York. 191, 192, 225, 619,
   651, 685–687, 691, 692
HARDER, ROLF; Montreal. 331
HARSHFIELD, KEN; Dallas. 503
HAÜY/BILLEBEAU/TOSETTO; Paris. 539
HAYES, J. MICHAEL; New York. 486
HAYS, PHILIP; New York. 709
HAZELTINE, BOBBIE; Houston, Tex. 765
HEDGES, BILL; Toronto, Ont. 530, 606
HEIMALL, ROBERT L.; New York. 714, 727
HELBLING, PETER; Zürich. 896–903
HENDERSON, DICK; Atlanta, Ga. 318
HÉRITIER, ROBERT; Lutry/SWI. 819, 820
HERMAN, SIDNEY; Cambridge, Mass. 335
HERRING, JERRY; Dallas. 501, 502, 547
HESS AND/OR ANTUPIT; New York. 556, 559, 561
HESS, RICHARD; New York. 592, 604
HIESTAND, E + U; Zürich. 815
HILL, WILLIAM; Dallas. 503
HINSCH, RENI; Hamburg. 640, 681–684, 857
HIRSCHBERGER, ROBERT; Braunschweig. 32–34,
   788
HOFER, JOSEF; Götzis/AUS. 207
HOFFMAN, EUGENE; Denver. 175, 204–206, 573
HOFFMANN, SANDY; New York. 479
HOLLER, STEVE; Rochester, N.Y. 799
HOLMES, DAVID; London. 225
HÖSLI, ROBERT; Zollikon/SWI. 278
HOUSE OF HARLEY, ART DEPT.; New York. 802,
   803
HUBLEY, FAITH; New York. 887–895
HUBLEY, JOHN; New York. 887–895
HUDSON, PAT; Bloomfield Hills, Mich. 237, 238,
   241
HUGHES, RON; Denver. 715
HUGUET, ENRIC; Barcelona. 189, 190, 325
HUKE, HEINZ; Langenhagen/GER. 732, 736
HUMM, FELIX; Milan. 229
HUSSMANN, HEINRICH; Rodenkirchen/GER. 663

IHNATOWICZ, MARIA; Warsaw. 146, 148, 153
IKEDA, SHUICHI; Tokyo. 807
ILIPRANDI, GIANCARLO; Milan. 88
ISAKA, YOSHITARO; Tokyo. 46

JACOB, FRANZ; Bruxelles. 301, 302
JACOBS, JIM; Dallas. 336, 337, 503
JAFFAN, AHMAD; Damascus. 112
JÄHN, HANNES; Köln. 642
JANIS, RICHARD; Toronto, Ont. 745
JANOWSKI, WITOLD; Warsaw. 79
JEANMART, CLAUDE; Balma/FRA. 851
JERVIS, PAUL; New York. 260
JOHNSON, DENNIS; Philadelphia, Pa. 296
JORDAN, PHIL; Washington, D.C. 220, 614
JOST, HEINZ; Bern. 149–152
JRIMKESS, LOU; Los Angeles. 35
JÜSP; Basel. 577

KANAI, KIYOSHI; New York. 775
KANO, DON; Los Angeles. 932–939
KATZ, JOEL; New Haven, Conn. 82
KELLER, PIERRE; Gilly/SWI. 83
KEMBLE, PETER; Cambridge, Mass. 42
KEMÉNY, GYÖRGY; Budapest. 4, 5, 16, 145
KEPKE, HERBERT; New York. 322
KEYSER, FRANS; Bruxelles. 327, 328

KIESER, GÜNTHER; Frankfurt/M. 95, 96, 494, 495,
   497, 498
KIMPTON, DAVID; Mexico-City. 44
KLARWEIN, MATI; New York. 718
KLECKNER, VALERIE; New York. 454, 455, 461,
   462, 473, 474
KLÖCKNER TEAM; Duisburg. 209–211
KNABENHANS, HELMUT; Pully/SWI. 598
KNER, ANDREW; New York. 38
KNÉZY, CLAUS; Zürich. 313
KOCK, CARL; Chicago. 664, 665
KOHLER, PIERRE; Toronto, Ont. 793
KOLOZSVÁRY, GEORG; Budapest. 124
KÖNIG, PAUL; Hildesheim/GER. 579
KOPRIVA, MILAN; Prag. 139
KOR, PAUL; Tel Aviv. 177
KOTILAINEN, AARNE; Rinnetie Mankkaa/FIN. 643
KOUDELKA, JOSEF; Prag. 139
KRAFT, HELMUT; Bad Hersfeld/GER. 66
KRAJEWSKI, ANDRZEJ; Warsaw. 130, 133, 135,
   136, 588, 591
KRAMER, MILLER, LOMDEN, GLASSMAN;
   Philadelphia, Pa. 847
KRAVEC, JOE; Pittsburgh, Pa. 230
KUSHNER, ARNOLD; New York. 458
KUSKE, ECKHARD; Braunschweig. 785, 786, 856
KUTIL, PAUL; New York. 478
KYSAR, ED; Los Angeles. 394, 395, 932–939

LaFLEUR, JACKIE; USA. 476
LALIBERTE; New York. 714
LAMBETH, ROD; Houston, Tex. 765
LANE, TONY; San Francisco. 725
LARGE, FRED; Los Angeles. 782
LaWARRE, BILL; Cincinnati, Ohio. 527
LAWRENCE, JACOB; New York. 599
LECLERC, JACQUES; Paris. 800
LEE, CLARENCE; Honolulu. 543
LEES, JOHN; Cambridge, Mass. 396, 413
LEFOLL, ALAIN; Paris. 265
LEHMAN, ACY; New York. 726
LEHNEN, JACQUES; Dübendorf/SWI. 409
LEMERY, GENE; Boston. 440
LEMOINE, GEORGES; Bonneuil/FRA. 324, 423–429,
   434–438, 810, 811
LENGERER, GRET; Stuttgart. 843
LENICA, JAN; Paris. 132, 585, 586
LEONE, ANTHONY V.; Philadelphia, Pa. 245, 246
LePREVOST, JOHN; Los Angeles. 735
LESSER, GILBERT; New York. 599
LEU, OLAF; Oberstedten/GER. 72, 193, 194
LEUPIN, HERBERT; Basel. 8, 101
LEWIS, TIM; New York. 77, 421, 422, 852
LICHTENSTEIN, ROY; New York. 154
LIEBERSON, GODDARD; USA. 853
LOOS, ADRIAN, DESIGN STUDIO; Los Angeles. 742
LOPEZ, ANTONIO; New York. 18, 19
LORTET, JACQUES; Vernon/FRA. 633
LUBALIN, HERB; New York. 188
LUCCI, GIUSEPPE; New York. 613
LUZZATI, EMANUELE; Gènes/ITA. 116

MACK, STAN; New York. 289
MALAST, MARGARET; New York. 754
MALONEY, PAT; Tiburon, Calif. 214
MANDEL, SAUL; Jericho, N.Y. 268
MANTEL, RICHARD; New York. 716
MANZI, RICCARDO; Milan. 676
MARAZZI, GIANNI; Milan. 787
MARCUS, BARRY; New York. 778, 779
MARI, ENZO; Milan. 374–376
MARK, MONA; New York. 473, 474
MARSHALL, DANIEL; New York. 773, 774
MARSHUTZ, ROGER; Los Angeles. 513
MARTIN, HAL; Chicago. 223
MARTIN, JEROME; New York. 273
MAS, GILBERT; Le Pecq/FRA. 57
MASSEY, JOHN; Chicago. 179, 180
MATELDI, BRUNETTA; Milan. 20, 859

MATHER, ARIELLE; Cambridge, Mass. 335
MAX, PETER; New York. 52, 53, 695, 696
McCARTY, JOHN; Seattle, Wa. 460
McCONNELL, JOHN; London. 860
McGINNIS, GEORGE; Ridgewood, N.J. 751
McMILLAN, WILLIAM; Arlington, Va. 563
McMULLAN, JAMES; New York. 249, 250, 285,
   356, 358, 570, 596, 778, 779
McPHAIL, JERRY; Dallas. 503
MEEK, JOHN; London. 430, 431, 441, 442
MEICHTRY, EGON; Zürich. 311, 312
MENUSY, CYLA; Tel Aviv. 143
MEYEROWITZ, RICK; New York. 725
MIHO, JAMES; New York. 511
MIHO, TOMOKO; New York. 511
MILLER, THEODORE; Philadelphia, Pa. 847
MILLIGAN, JOHN; White Plains, N.Y. 402, 403
MITCHELL, ERROL; Macclesfield, Cheshire/GB.
   355, 357
MIZAK, RON; Pittsburgh, Pa. 399
MORGAN, JONATHAN D.; Leeds/GB. 777
MORGAN, MIKE; Atlanta, Ga. 199
MORISHIMA, HIROSHI; Los Angeles. 35
MORLIOHEM, PHILIPPE; Paris. 213
MOSINSKI, MAREK; Katowice/POL. 91
MOUNT, REGINALD; London. 64
MUNSTERHJELM, MARIA; Helsinki. 1

NAGAI, KAZUMASA; Tokyo. 756
NAIKI, MIKE; New York. 707
NÉAMA, MAY; Anvers. 323, 349, 479
NEGRI, ILIO; Milan. 267, 832
NEUMANN, HANS-D.; Hannover. 506, 507
NEWTON, DAVID; London. 307
NEWTON, WILLIAM; Toronto, Ont. 530, 606
NILES, DAVID; Boston. 440
NIMETH, BRIAN; Cleveland, Ohio. 286, 287
NITTNER, TOMAS; New York. 762
NOLAN, MARY; Chicago. 443
NONEMAN, JOHN; New York. 102
NONEMAN, PATRICIA; New York. 102
NORMAN, DEREK; Chicago. 855
NOVAK, JAY; Los Angeles. 513, 626
NYSTRÖM, P.O.; Helsinki. 65

ODGERS, JAMES; Manhattan Beach, Calif. 414
OEHRING, HANS-GEORG; Braunschweig. 785,
   786, 856
OERTER, FRITZ HENRY; Nürnberg/GER. 99
OHASHI, TADASHI; Tokyo. 201–203, 827, 828
OHCHI, HIROSHI; Tokyo. 789, 830
OHLSSON, ESKIL; New York. 740
OIKAWA, MASAMICHI; Tokyo. 121–123
OLDANI, BRUNO; Oslo. 555, 557, 558
OLIVER, BILL; Philadelphia, Pa. 417–419
OLPE, PETER; Basel. 111
OMENAMÄKI, OSMO; Helsinki. 37
ONEGIN, ANDRZEJ; Warsaw. 142
OSBORN, STEPHEN; Palo Alto, Calif. 658, 659, 861
OSTERWALDER, HANS-ULRICH; Kilchberg/SWI.
   182, 251, 252
OSTERWALDER, UTE; Kilchberg/SWI. 251, 252
OTTIGER, WALTER; Bern. 580

PACEY, MICHAEL; Los Angeles. 749
PAGANUCCI, BOB; New York. 404, 405, 411, 412,
   421, 422
PALLADINI, DAVID; New York. 361–363
PARKER, AL; Carmel Valley, Calif. 634
PECKOLICK, ALAN; New York. 754
PEDERSEN, SHARLEEN; Woodland Hill, Calif. 712
PEDERSON, MARTIN; New York. 613
PERRET, PAUL ANDRÉ; Lausanne. 598
PERRY, JUDY; New York. 482
PFÄFFLI, BRUNO; Arcueil/FRA. 247
PIATTI, CELESTINO; Basel. 2, 97, 575
PICASSO, PABLO; Avignon/FRA. 491
PINTÉR, FERENC; Milan. 677, 689
PIPER, CHR.; Essen-Bredeney. 92, 127, 488, 492

Index to Art Directors
Verzeichnis der Künstlerischen Leiter
Index des directeurs artistiques

Index to Agencies and Studios
Verzeichnis der Agenturen und Studios
Index des agences et studios

Index to Advertisers
Verzeichnis der Auftraggeber
Index des clients

1

Posters

Plakate

Affiches

Posters / Plakate / Affiches

1) Poster for autumn fashion fabrics sold in the stores of the SOK organization. Full colour. (FIN)
2) Polychrome poster for cigarillos. (SWI)
3) Poster for fruit juices. Red apple, green leaf. (SWI)
4) Poster for a brand of cigarettes. (HUN)
5) 'Old star—new star!' Poster for a new soft drink. Bright colours on yellow ground. (HUN)
6) Pop poster for a make of shoes. Polychrome. (SWI)
7) Poster for a boutique in Zurich. Black and white. (SWI)
8) Poster for cigarettes (the brand name means 'red hand'). (GER)
9) Humorous poster for *Coco Wheats*, with nine examples of outstanding failures. (USA)

1) Plakat einer Warenhauskette, die Stoffe für die Herbstmode anbietet. Kräftige, lebhafte Farben. (FIN)
2) Plakat in dunklen Brauntönen für Zigarillos. (SWI)
3) Plakat für Obstsäfte. Roter Apfel, grünes Blatt. (SWI)
4) Zigaretten-Plakat des ungarischen Tabak-Gewerbes. (HUN)
5) «Alter Stern – neuer Stern!». Plakat für ein neues Erfrischungsgetränk. Grelle Farben auf gelbem Grund. (HUN)
6) Pop-Plakat, mehrfarbig, für eine Schuhmarke. (SWI)
7) Plakat eines Modegeschäftes für junge Leute. (SWI)
8) Plakat der Firma Roth-Händle in Lahr für Zigaretten. (GER)
9) Humoristisches Plakat für «Schokolade-Getreideflocken» mit neun Beispielen von merkwürdigen Misserfolgen. (USA)

Artist | Künstler | Artiste:

1) MARIA MUNSTERHJELM/MARJATTA ARANTILA
2) CELESTINO PIATTI
3) EMANUEL BOSSHART
4) 5) GYÖRGY KEMÉNY
6) LISBETH WESSBECHER
7) HANS ULRICH
8) HERBERT LEUPIN
9) MILTON GLASER

1) Affiches pour des tissus d'automne, en vente dans les magasins SOK. Polychrome. (FIN)
2) Affiche en couleur pour des cigarillos. (SWI)
3) Affiche pour des jus de fruits. Polychrome. (SWI)
4) Affiche pour une marque de cigarettes. (HUN)
5) «Vieille étoile – nouvelle étoile!» Affiche pour une nouvelle boisson rafraîchissante. Polychrome. (HUN)
6) Affiche «pop» pour une marque de chaussures. (SWI)
7) Affiche pour une boutique «jeune». Noir et blanc. (SWI)
8) Affiche pour une marque de cigarettes. (GER)
9) Affiche humoristique pour des flocons de céréales au chocolat. (USA)

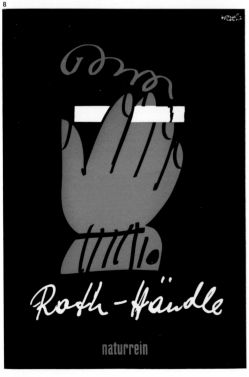

Art Director | Directeur artistique:

1) TORSTI PENTTINEN
2) CELESTINO PIATTI
4) SÁNDORNÉ SIK
5) ERIKA BAKTAY
6) ROLAND BAERTSCH
8) HERBERT LEUPIN
9) PETER COUTROULIS

Agency | Agentur | Agence – Studio:

6) BAERTSCH, MURER + RUCKSTUHL, ZÜRICH
7) KREATIV-TEAM ULRICH + FEHLMANN, ZÜRICH
9) HURVIS, BINZER & CHURCHILL, INC., CHICAGO/PUSH PIN STUDIOS, INC., NEW YORK

10

11

14

10) 11) Two hippie-inspired, popular posters for a distillery. (NLD)
12) Poster for a Swiss brewers' association, offered as a gift on request. (SWI)
13) Poster in the style of an old painting for a coffee extract. (SWI)
14) Poster for a table water in nine-colour offset (figure in dull orange-vermilion, background rose). (FRA)
15) Poster for a New York fashion stylist. Two reds and yellow. (USA)

10) 11) Plakate im Hippie-Stil für D. Visser und Zonen, Schiedam, Distillerie. (NLD)
12) Plakat des Schweizerischen Bierbrauervereins, Zürich, das auf Anfrage gratis abgegeben wurde. (SWI)
13) Plakat im Stil eines alten Gemäldes für die Thomi und Franck AG, Basel. (SWI)
14) Neunfarbiges Plakat für ein Tafelgetränk. Figur Orange auf rosa Grund. (FRA)
15) Plakat für einen New Yorker Modeschöpfer. Zwei Rottöne und Gelb. (USA)

10) 11) Affiches d'inspiration hippie, pour une distillerie. (NLD)
12) Affiche de l'Association des brasseurs suisses, distribuée gratuitement. (SWI)
13) Affiche exécutée dans le style d'un tableau ancien, pour la Thomi & Franck SA, Bâle. (SWI)
14) Affiche en neuf couleurs de la Société Fermière, Vichy. (FRA)
15) Affiche pour un dessinateur de mode. Deux tons de rouge et jaune. (USA)

Artist | Künstler | Artiste:

10) 11) A.A. STOCK
12) ELVIRA VOMSTEIN
13) CLÉMENT DÉPRÈS
14) BERNARD VILLEMOT
15) STANISLAW ZAGORSKI

Art Director | Directeur artistique:

10) 11) A.A. STOCK
13) GGK AG, BASEL

Agency | Agentur | Agence – Studio:

10) 11) PUBLI STUDIO, SCHIEDAM/NLD
12) WERBEAGENTUR HÖRNER, ZÜRICH
13) GGK AG, BASEL
14) HAVAS CONSEIL, PARIS

**Posters / Plakate
Affiches**

12

13

15

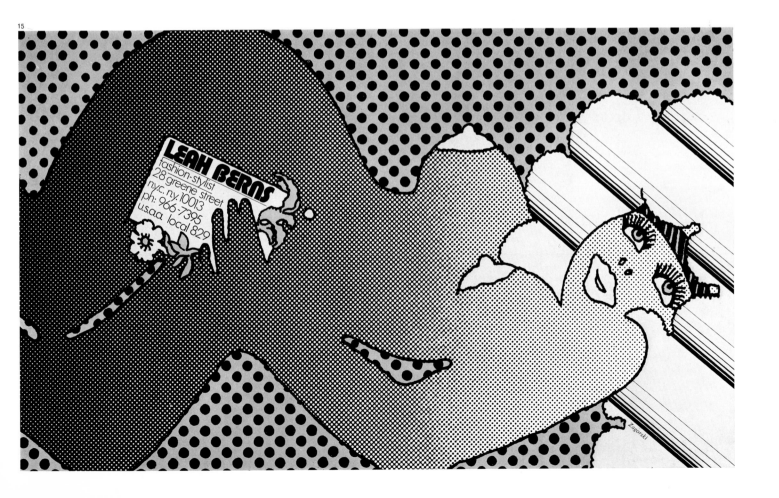

16

The ones who have it, can't do without it.

17

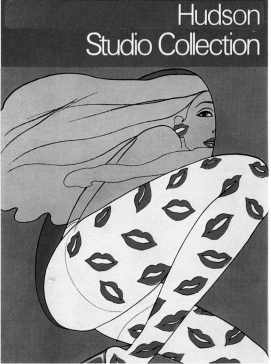

18　　19

35

39

Artist | Künstler | Artiste:

32)–34) ROBERT HISCHBERGER
35) HIROSHI MORISHIMA/
CARL SELTZER/
LOU JRIMKESS
36) SADEGH BARIRANI
37) OSMO OMENAMÄKI
38) ISADORE SELTZER/
ANDREW KNER
39) RAYMOND BERTRAND/
H. VON SYDOW-ZIRKWITZ
40) MINORU TAKAHASHI
41) WALTER VELEZ

Art Director | Directeur artistique:

32)–34) WILHELM BETTGES
36) SADEGH BARIRANI
38) ANDREW KNER
39) H. VON SYDOW-ZIRKWITZ
40) MINORU TOKAHASHI
41) RUBY B. MAZUR

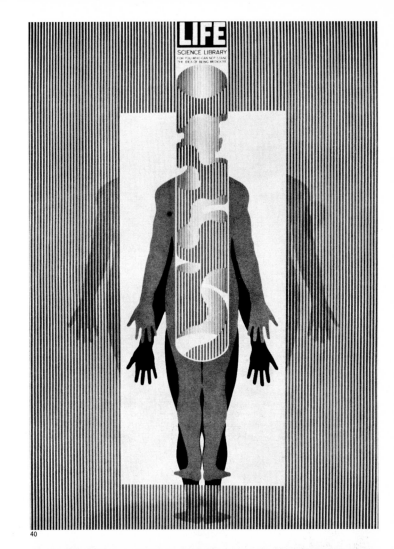

40

41

32)–34) Série d'affiches pour le supplément dominical illustré
d'un quotidien. (GER)
35) Affiche pour une exposition d'art publicitaire japonais à
Los Angeles. Sceau doré, soleil rouge. (USA)
36) Affiche pour une semaine de propagande en faveur du livre.
Polychrome sur fond bleu. (IRN)
37) Affiche pour un imprimeur en sérigraphie. (FIN)
38) Affiche en couleur du THE NEW YORK TIMES, destinée à
encourager la lecture en vacances. (USA)
39) Affiche pour une galerie d'art érotique. Langue rouge. (GER)
40) Affiche pour la bibliothèque scientifique de LIFE. (JAP)
41) Affiche pour un enregistrement *Paramount* d'une formation
«beat». Polychrome. (USA)

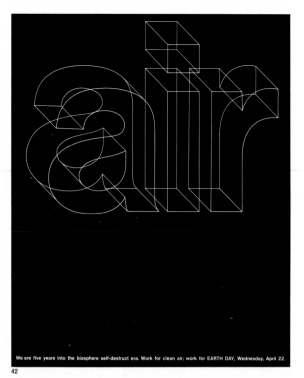

We are five years into the biosphere self-destruct era. Work for clean air; work for EARTH DAY, Wednesday, April 22.

42

DATSUN GIVES YOU SOMETHING EXXTRA

43

Artist | Künstler | Artiste:

42) PETER KEMBLE
43) TERESA WOODWARD/TOM WOODWARD
44) DAVID KIMPTON/MICHAEL TECHON
45) ENRIC SATUÉ
46) YOSHITARO ISAKA
47) MILTON GLASER

Art Director | Directeur artistique:

42) PETER KEMBLE
43) GARY PRIESTER
44) MICHAEL TECHON
45) ENRIC SATUÉ
47) GIORGIO SOAVI

espectacles juvenils

45

46

Agency | Agentur | Agence – Studio:

42) DESIGNS & DEVICES, BOSTON, MASS.
43) PARKER ADVERTISING, INC., PALOS VERDES, CALIF.
44) PENTHOUSE STUDIOS, MEXICO
45) ENRIC SATUÉ, BARCELONA
47) UFFICIO PUBBLICITÀ OLIVETTI, MILAN

Posters / Plakate / Affiches

42) Poster in favour of a cleaner environment. White on blue. (USA)
43) Showroom poster for *Datsun* cars. Hand in colour. (USA)
44) Billboard poster in twelve sections for ICI paints. (MEX)
45) Poster for 'Magic Dragon', an enterprise for audiovisual shows for children. Showy colours. (SPA)
46) 47) Two posters for a new *Olivetti* typewriter. (ITA)

42) Plakat zugunsten einer saubereren Umwelt. Weiss auf Blau. (USA)
43) Innenplakat eines Ausstellungsraumes für *Datsun*-Fahrzeuge. Ärmel orange mit gelben und blauen Sternen, Hand rosa mit gelben Fingernägeln, Grund weiss. (USA)
44) Zwölfteiliges Landstrassen-Plakat für ICI Farben. (MEX)
45) Plakat in frischen Farben für den «Zauberdrachen», ein Unternehmen für audio-visuelle Vorführungen für Kinder. (SPA)
46) 47) Zwei Plakate für die Schreibmaschine *Valentine* von *Olivetti*. (ITA)

42) Affiche pour la propreté de l'environnement. Blanc sur bleu. (USA)
43) Affiche d'intérieur pour les voitures *Datsun*. Manche orange à étoiles jaunes et bleues, main rose aux ongles jaunes, fond blanc. (USA)
44) Affiche à douze panneaux, posée le long des grandes routes, en faveur des couleurs ICI. (MEX)
45) Affiche de couleurs vives pour le «Dragon magique», une entreprise de présentations audio-visuelles pour les enfants. (SPA)
46) 47) Affiches pour les machines à écrire *Olivetti*. (ITA)

48

49

48) 49) 'Saving is fun at the children's counter of the Banque Populaire Suisse.' A bank's colourful gift posters to stimulate saving in children. (SWI)
50) 'Sudden rushing into the road is the cause of accidents.' Safety poster. (POL)
51) Poster to persuade children to decide for the nursing professions. (USA)
52) Poster for the Chelsea National Bank. (USA)
53) Poster against smoking issued by the American Cancer Society. (USA)
54) Post Office poster to persuade people to pack parcels properly. (GB)

48) 49) Mehrfarbige Gratisplakate der Schweizerischen Volksbank. (SWI)
50) Plakat für Verkehrssicherheit der Civic Militia, Warschau. (POL)
51) «Hilf um zu wachsen – wachse um zu helfen». Plakat, das sich an Kinder wendet, um in ihnen den Wunsch nach einem Pflegeberuf reifen zu lassen. (USA)
52) Plakat einer Bank. (USA)
53) «Anti-Raucher»-Plakat einer Gesellschaft zur Krebsverhütung. (USA)
54) Plakat der englischen Postverwaltung für gut und sauber verpackte Pakete. (GB)

48) 49) Affiche polychrome, distribuée gratuitement aux enfants, pour les carnets d'épargne de la Banque Populaire Suisse. (SWI)
50) Affiche en faveur de la sécurité routière. (POL)
51) «Aide à grandir – grandis pour aider». Affiche destinée à encourager les enfants à choisir la profession d'infirmier ou d'infirmière. (USA)
52) Affiche pour une banque. (USA)
53) Affiche «anti-tabac» d'une société de lutte contre le cancer. (USA)
54) Affiche des postes britanniques, recommandant au public de bien emballer les colis. (GB)

51

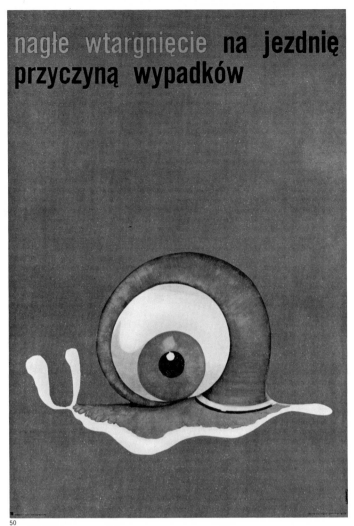

50

53

52

54

Art Director / Directeur artistique:

50) GUSTAW MAJEWSKI
52) 53) PETER MAX
54) D. EWERS

Agency / Agentur / Agence — Studio:

50) WAG, WARSAW
52) 53) PETER MAX ENTERPRISES, NEW YORK

Posters/Plakate/Affiches

Johann Sebastian Bach

55

57

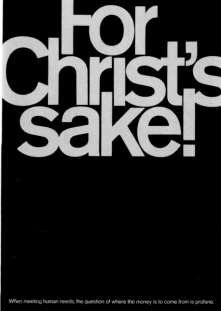

61

56

**Posters / Plakate
Affiches**

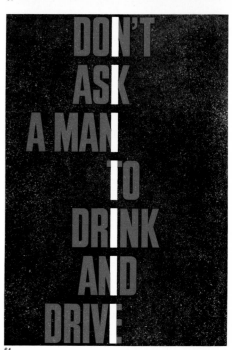

64

40

słowa sobie   czyny sobie

58

GERMAN PROFILES

WILLY BRANDT

59

America the beautiful.

60

HELLAS   21 APR. 67

62

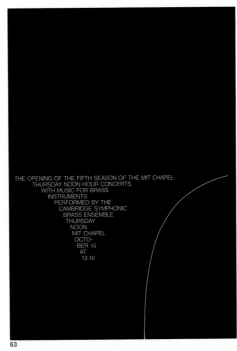

THE OPENING OF THE FIFTH SEASON OF THE MIT CHAPEL
THURSDAY NOON HOUR CONCERTS
WITH MUSIC FOR BRASS
INSTRUMENTS
PERFORMED BY THE
CAMBRIDGE SYMPHONIC
BRASS ENSEMBLE
THURSDAY
NOON
MIT CHAPEL
OCTO-
BER 15
AT
12:10

63

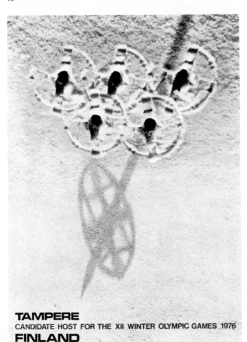

TAMPERE
CANDIDATE HOST FOR THE XII WINTER OLYMPIC GAMES 1976
FINLAND

65

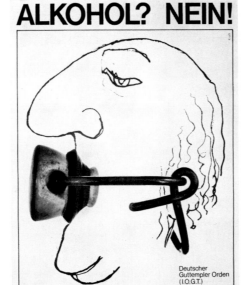

ALKOHOL? NEIN!

Deutscher
Guttempler Orden
(I.O.G.T.)

81. GUTTEMPLERTAGUNG
BAD HERSFELD 7-11.5.'70

66

55) 59) Posters from a campaign to create goodwill for West Germany in the United States. Fig. 59 is a vacuum-formed plastic poster about the German Chancellor. (GER)
56) Poster offered as a gift to young couples opening an account with a bank. (DEN)
57) Poster for an audiovisual festival in Frankfurt. (FRA)
58) 'Words on the one hand – deeds on the other.' Educative social poster. (POL)
60) Poster against environmental pollution. Full colour. (USA)
61) Poster for Broadway United Church of Christ to encourage giving for the needy. Black and white. (USA)
62) Political poster against military government in Greece. Black and red. (GER)
63) Poster for a concert of music for brass instruments at the Massachusetts Institute of Technology. (USA)
64) Small poster against the abuse of alcohol. (GB)
65) Poster supporting Tampere's candidature for the 1976 Winter Olympic Games. Blue shadow. (FIN)
66) Poster for a temperance society. Black and white. (GER)

55) 59) Plakate aus einer Good-Will-Kampagne für Westdeutschland in den Vereinigten Staaten. Fig. 59 ist ein Plastik-Plakat und zeigt das Portrait des Bundeskanzlers. (GER)
56) Plakat einer Bank, die es jungen Paaren bei der Eröffnung eines Bankkontos als Geschenk überreicht. (DEN)
57) Plakat für ein audiovisuelles Festival in Frankfurt. (FRA)
58) «Hier Worte – dort Taten». Sozialkritisches Plakat. (POL)
60) In kräftigen Farben gehaltenes Plakat, das zum Kampf gegen die Luftverschmutzung aufruft. (USA)
61) Schwarzweisses Plakat einer christlichen Gemeinde, das um Unterstützung der Bedürftigen bittet. (USA)
62) Politisches Plakat, das sich gegen die Militärregierung in Griechenland richtet. Schwarz und rot. (GER)
63) Plakat für ein Blasmusik-Konzert. (USA)
64) Kleinplakat gegen den Missbrauch von Alkohol. (GB)
65) Plakat zur Unterstützung der Kandidatur von Tampere für die Winter-Olympiade von 1976. (FIN)
66) Schwarzweisses Abstinenzler-Plakat des Deutschen Guttempler-Ordens. (GER)

55) 59) Affiches d'une campagne de sympathie menée aux Etats-Unis en faveur de l'Allemagne de l'Ouest. L'ill. 59 est un portrait plastifié du chancelier fédéral. (GER)
56) Affiche d'une banque, offerte gracieusement aux jeunes mariés qui y ouvrent un compte. (DEN)
57) Affiche pour un festival audiovisuel à Francfort. (FRA)
58) «D'un côté des mots – de l'autre des actes». Affiche socio-éducative. (POL)
60) Affiche pour la lutte contre la pollution de l'air. Polychrome. (USA)
61) Affiche d'une association religieuse, en faveur de l'aide aux nécessiteux. Noir et blanc. (USA)
62) Affiche politique, dirigée contre le gouvernement militaire en Grèce. Noir et rouge. (GER)
63) Affiche pour un concert d'instruments à vent. (USA)
64) Affichette contre l'abus d'alcool. (GB)
65) Affiche soutenant la candidature de Tampere pour les Jeux Olympiques d'hiver 1976. (FIN)
66) Affiche d'une société de tempérance. Noir et blanc. (GER)

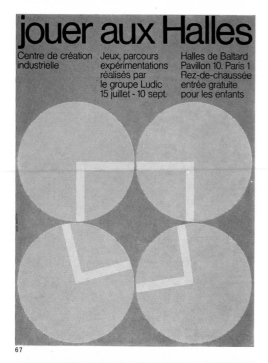

67

68

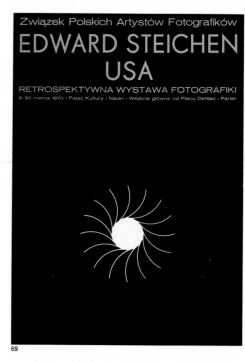

69

70

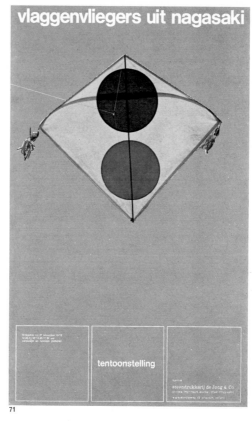

71

72

67) 68) Posters in fluorescent colours for exhibitions (subjects: games and the table) organized by a centre of industrial design. (FRA)

69) Poster for a retrospective exhibition of the work of an American photographer. Black and white. (POL)

70) 71) 'Children draw children' (black and white, red print) and 'Flag kites of Nagasaki' (kite in colour on pale blue ground). Two posters for exhibitions staged by the printer de Jong & Co. (NLD)

72) Poster for an international exhibition of drugs and cosmetics in Frankfurt. (GER)

73) Poster for Iran's first film festival. Silk-screen. (IRN)

74) Poster issued by the Vietnam Moratorium Committee. (USA)

67) 68) Plakate in Leuchtfarben für Ausstellungen einer Gruppe für industrielle Formgebung. (FRA)

69) Schwarzweisses Plakat für eine Ausstellung über das Werk eines amerikanischen Photographen. (POL)

70) 71) «Kinder zeichnen Kinder» (schwarzweiss mit roter Schrift) und «Drachenflaggen über Nagasaki» (Drache farbig auf hellblauem Grund). Zwei Plakate für die Ausstellungen eines Druckers. (NLD)

72) Plakat der Messe- und Ausstellungsgesellschaft in Frankfurt. (GER)

73) Siebdruck-Plakat in Pastellfarben für ein Festival von Film-Erstaufführungen in Iran. (IRN)

74) Plakat des Vietnam Moratorium-Komitees. (USA)

67) 68) Affiches pour des expositions au Centre de création industrielle, Paris. (FRA)

69) Affiche pour une exposition rétrospective des œuvres d'un photographe américain. Noir et blanc. (POL)

70) 71) «Des enfants dessinent des enfants» (noir et blanc, texte en rouge) et «Les cerfs-volants de Nagasaki» (cerf-volant en couleur sur fond bleu ciel). Affiches pour des expositions organisées par un imprimeur. (NLD)

72) Affiche pour une exposition internationale de produits pharmaceutiques et cosmétiques. (GER)

73) Affiche pour un festival cinématographique. Sérigraphie en teintes pastels. (IRN)

74) Affiche du Comité moratoire du Vietnam. (USA)

Artist | Künstler | Artiste:

67) 68) JEAN WIDMER
69) TOMASZ RUMINSKI
70) 71) PIETER BRATTINGA/DICK BRUNA
72) JOSSE GOFFIN/OLAF LEU
73) SADEGH BARIRANI
74) IVAN CHERMAYEFF

Art Director | Directeur artistique:

69) URBANOWICZ HENRYK
72) OLAF LEU
73) SADEGH BARIRANI
74) IVAN CHERMAYEFF

73

"Doves of All Nations" Ivan Chermayeff © 1970

74

Agency | Agentur | Agence – Studio:

72) WEST MEDIA, BAD HOMBURG/GER
73) CULTURE AND ARTS ADM., TEHERAN
74) CHERMAYEFF & GEISMAR ASSOC., INC., NEW YORK

Posters / Plakate / Affiches

75

76

75) Poster for an annual agricultural fair. (SWI)
76) Poster for an exhibition of the artist's work in Paris. (FRA)
77) Poster announcing a move of the *Rob Roy* clothing stores. (USA)
78) 79) Posters from a series for the Polish circus. (POL)
80) Poster for an exhibition in Frankfurt. Bright colours on wings. (GER)
81) Poster for a concert of contemporary music in Berlin. Black and red. (GER)

75) Plakat für die alljährliche Land- und Milchwirtschaftsmesse in St. Gallen. (SWI)
76) Plakat für die Ausstellung der Werke eines Künstlers. (FRA)
77) Plakat zur Anzeige des Domizilwechsels eines Modegeschäftes. (USA)
78) 79) Zwei mehrfarbige Plakate aus einer Serie für den polnischen Zirkus. (POL)
80) Plakat des Freien Deutschen Hochstiftes in Frankfurt für eine Clemens-Brentano-Ausstellung. Schwarzweiss, auf den Flügeln farbige Verzierungen. (GER)
81) Plakat des Senders Freies Berlin für ein Konzert zeitgenössischer Musik. Rot und schwarz. (GER)

75) Affiche pour une foire agricole annuelle. (SWI)
76) Affiche pour une exposition des œuvres de l'artiste à Paris. (FRA)
77) Affiche annonçant le changement d'adresse d'une maison de confection. (USA)
78) 79) Affiches tirées d'une série en faveur du cirque national polonais. (POL)
80) Affiche pour une exposition à Francfort. Noir et blanc, enjolivures en couleurs vives sur les ailes. (GER)
81) Affiche pour un concert de musique contemporaine à Berlin. Noir et rouge. (GER)

77

Posters / Plakate / Affiches

Artist | Künstler | Artiste:

75) ROMANO CHICHERIO
76) ANDRÉ FRANÇOIS
77) TIM LEWIS
78) MACIEJ URBANIEC
79) WITOLD JANOWSKI
80) KRISTIAN ROTH
81) HANS FÖRTSCH/SIGRID VON BAUMGARTEN

78

80

79

81

Art Director | Directeur artistique:

75) ROMANO CHICHERIO
77) ALBERT BEHAR
78) 79) GUSTAW MAJEWSKI
80) KRISTIAN ROTH
81) HANS FÖRTSCH/SIGRID VON BAUMGARTEN

Agency | Agentur | Agence – Studio:

75) STUDIO GRAFICO ROMANO CHICHERIO, LUGANO
77) ALBERT BEHAR ADVERTISING, NEW YORK
78) 79) WAG, WARSAW
81) HANS FÖRTSCH/SIGRID VON BAUMGARTEN, BERLIN

Artist | Künstler | Artiste:

82) JOEL KATZ
83) PIERRE KELLER
84) 85) HEINRICH BRANDT
86) ALLAN D'ARCANGELO
87) IRIS VOM HOF
88) GIANCARLO ILIPRANDI
89) MALCOLM WADDELL
90) JUKKA VEISTOLA/JUSSI POTERI/KYÖSTY VARIS

Art Director | Directeur artistique:

82) JOEL KATZ
83) MAX ALTORFER
84) 85) HEINRICH BRANDT
87) IRIS VOM HOF
88) GIANCARLO ILIPRANDI
90) JUKKA VEISTOLA/JUSSI POTERI/KYÖSTY VARIS

83

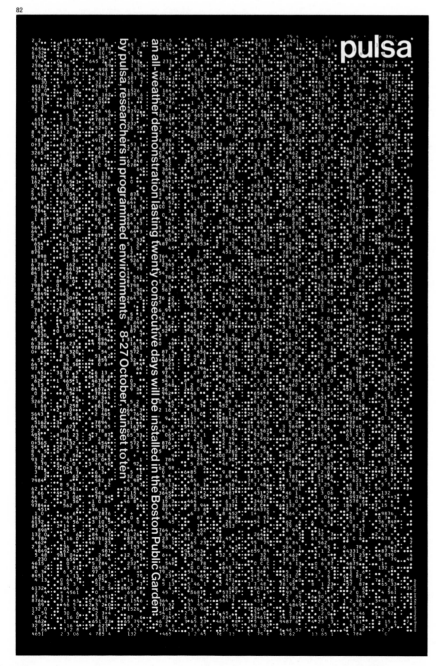

82

87

Agency | Agentur | Agence – Studio:

82) JOEL KATZ, NEW HAVEN, CONN.
84) 85) HEINRICH BRANDT, DÜSSELDORF-BENRATH
87) PRESSE- UND WERBEAMT, WUPPERTAL/GER
89) KARELIA INTERNATIONAL, ONTARIO
90) VARIKSEN TOIMISTO, HELSINKI

Posters / Plakate / Affiches

31.10.'70 17 Uhr **Reformationsfeier**
Rheinhalle
Düsseldorf

Unser Glaube in der Wirrnis unserer Zeit

Evangelischer
Arbeitsausschuß
Düsseldorf

Prof. D. Dr. Wilhelm Niesel
Präsident des Reformierten Weltbundes

Neue geistliche Lieder
Kantorei Holthausen
Studio Combo Altstadt
Leitung
Siegfried Rediske

84

15.3.'70 17 Uhr **Christen bekennen sich zum Kreuz**
Rheinhalle
Düsseldorf

Evangelischer
Kirchenkreisverband
und
der Katholikenausschuß
Düsseldorf

Es sprechen
Pater Dr. Mario von Galli, Zürich
Prof. D. Dr. Helmut Thielicke
Hamburg

85

86

88

finnish textiles from karelia international at the royal ontario museum 1st april–4th may 1969

89

90

82) Poster about a *Pulsa* light and sound demonstration in Boston. White and silver on black. (USA)
83) Poster for an exhibition on Swiss federal art scholarships. Two reds, white lettering. (SWI)
84) 85) Posters for religious meetings in Dusseldorf. Fluorescent colours on silver. (GER)
86) Poster for a festival in the Lincoln Center. (USA)
87) Poster for a concert of contemporary music. Purple and black. (GER)
88) Poster for an exhibition of graphic design in Milan on the theme of aggression and violence. (ITA)
89) Poster for an exhibition of Finnish textiles. (CAN)
90) Poster for a snake exhibition. (FIN)

82) Plakat für eine unter freiem Himmel und bei jedem Wetter durchgeführte Demonstration über Licht- und Ton-Installationen. Weiss und silber auf Schwarz. (USA)
83) Ausstellungsplakat. Zwei Rottöne, weisse Schrift. (SWI)
84) 85) Plakate für Vorträge zweier Konfessionen in Düsseldorf über religiöse Fragen. (GER)
86) Plakat für ein Festival in New York. (USA)
87) Plakat für ein Konzert zeitgenössischer Musik der Konzertgesellschaft Wuppertal. Violett und schwarz. (GER)
88) Plakat für eine Ausstellung graphischer Kunst über das Thema «Angriff und Gewalt». (ITA)
89) Ausstellungsplakat für finnische Stoffe. (CAN)
90) Plakat für eine gross angelegte Schlangenschau. (FIN)

82) Affiche pour une démonstration en plein air d'installations son et lumière. Blanc et argent sur noir. (USA)
83) Affiche pour une exposition consacrée aux bourses artistiques en Suisse. Deux rouges, texte en blanc. (SWI)
84) 85) Affiches pour des conférences religieuses à Dusseldorf. Couleurs fluorescentes sur argent. (GER)
86) Affiche pour un festival au Lincoln Center. (USA)
87) Affiche pour un concert de musique contemporaine. Mauve sur noir. (GER)
88) Affiche pour une exposition d'art graphique à Milan, sur le thème «Agression et violence». (ITA)
89) Affiche pour une exposition de tissus finlandais. (CAN)
90) Affiche pour une exposition de serpents. (FIN)

91

92

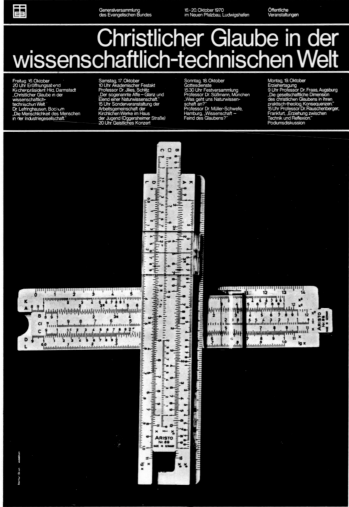

93

94

95

96

Artist / Künstler / Artiste:

91) MAREK MOSINSKI
92) CHRISTIAN PIPER
93) REINHART BRAUN
94) FRANCO GRIGNANI
95) 96) GÜNTHER KIESER
97) CELESTINO PIATTI

Art Director / Directeur artistique:

91) TADEUSZ GRABOWSKI
92) CHRISTIAN PIPER
93) REINHART BRAUN
94) GERNOT KRAMER
97) TH. BECK

97

91) Poster for a zoo in Chorzów. (POL)
92) Poster for a showing of films in a design school. Black on yellow, blue stars. (GER)
93) 'Christian faith in a scientific and technical world.' Poster for a religious meeting. (GER)
94) Poster for an exhibition of Italian graphic design in Karlsruhe. (GER)
95) Poster for a blues group. Full colour. (GER)
96) Poster for a concert. Full colour. (GER)
97) Poster for a programme of symphony concerts in Basle. Two reds on dark blue, white type matter. (SWI)

91) Plakat für einen zoologischen Garten. (POL)
92) Plakat für eine Filmvorführung der Volkwangschule für Gestaltung. Schwarz, gelb, Sterne blau. (GER)
93) Schwarzweisses Plakat des Evangelischen Bundes in Bensheim für ein religiöses Treffen. (GER)
94) Plakat für eine Karlsruher Ausstellung über graphische Kunst in Italien. (GER)
95) Plakat der Concert Büro GmbH, Frankfurt, für eine Blues-Gruppe. Mehrfarbig. (GER)
96) Mehrfarbiges Konzertplakat. (GER)
97) Plakat der Allgemeinen Musikgesellschaft Basel mit Programm für verschiedene Aufführungen von Symphonie-Konzerten. Zwei Rottöne auf dunkelblauem Grund, weisse Schrift. (SWI)

91) Affiche pour un jardin zoologique. (POL)
92) Affiche pour la présentation d'un film dans une école de design. Polychrome. (GER)
93) «La foi chrétienne dans un monde scientifique et technique». Affiche pour une réunion religieuse. (GER)
94) Affiche pour une exposition d'art graphique italien à Karlsruhe. (GER)
95) Affiche pour un concert de blues. Polychrome. (GER)
96) Affiche en couleur pour un concert. (GER)
97) Affiche montrant le programme de concerts symphoniques donnés à Bâle. Deux rouges sur bleu foncé, texte en blanc. (SWI)

Agency / Agentur / Agence – Studio:

91) WAG, WARSAW
92) CHRISTIAN PIPER, ESSEN, BREDENEY/GER
94) BERNHARD BURGER, KARLSRUHE

Posters / Plakate / Affiches

Posters / Plakate
Affiches

98) Poster for a German film comedy. Polychrome title. (CSR)
99) Poster for a toy museum in Nuremberg. Full colour. (GER)
100) Poster for an exhibition of children's books in Offenbach. Polychrome head. (GER)
101) Poster for a clown's circus performance. (SWI)
102) Poster for an exhibition of town planning in the Whitney Museum. Black and yellow. (USA)
103) Poster for an agricultural show. Orange, green, blue and dark brown. (CSR)
104) Poster for an ideal home exhibition. (ITA)
105) Poster for a Mozart week in Dusseldorf. Black-and-white design, coloured lettering. (GER)

98) Plakat für eine deutsche Filmkomödie. (CSR)
99) Farbiges Plakat der Stadt Nürnberg für das Spielzeugmuseum. (GER)
100) Plakat des Klingspor-Museums für die 15. internationale Bilderbuch-Ausstellung. Kopf mehrfarbig. (GER)
101) Zirkusplakat für die Darbietungen eines berühmten Clowns. (SWI)
102) Plakat für eine Ausstellung über Städteplanung in einem Museum. Schwarz und gelb auf weissem Grund. (USA)
103) Plakat für eine landwirtschaftliche Ausstellung. Orange, grün, blau und dunkelbraun. (CSR)
104) Plakat einer Wohnkultur-Ausstellung. (ITA)
105) Plakat der Deutschen Oper am Rhein in Düsseldorf für eine Mozart-Woche. Schwarzweisse Zeichnung, farbige Schrift. (GER)

Artist / Künstler / Artiste:

98) ZDENEK ZIEGLER
99) FRITZ HENRY OERTER
100) WILFRIED BLECHER
101) HERBERT LEUPIN
102) PATRICIA NONEMAN/JOHN NONEMAN
103) VACLAV RYKR
104) GIULIO CONFALONIERI
105) WALTER BREKER

Art Director / Directeur artistique:

99) FRITZ HENRY OERTER
100) DR. HANS A. HALBEY
101) HERBERT LEUPIN
102) PATRICIA NONEMAN
103) LIBUSE POUROVÁ
104) GIULIO CONFALONIERI

Agency / Agentur / Agence – Studio:

102) NONEMAN & NONEMAN, NEW YORK
103) CESKY FOND, USTI NAD LABEM / CSR

98

99

102

103

100

101

104

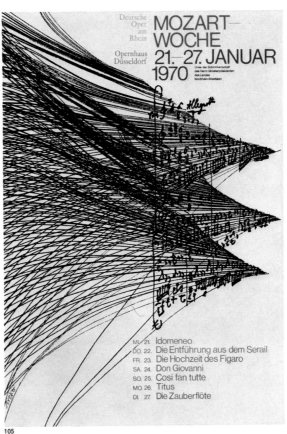

105

106

107

108

Posters / Plakate / Affiches

109

Artist / Künstler / Artiste:

130) 133) 135) 136) ANDRZEJ KRAJEWSKI
131) FRANCISZEK STAROWIEYSKI
132) JAN LENICA
134) WIKTOR GÓRKA

Art Director / Directeur artistique:

134) STANISLAWA STANISLAWSKA

130) Poster for a German film. (POL)
131) Poster for a French crime film. (POL)
132) Poster for a performance of Richard Strauss's *Elektra*. (POL)
133) Poster for a colour film (Angélique and the Sultan). (POL)
134) Poster for a Lehar operetta. Two greens and black. (POL)
135) Poster for an English film comedy (The Pink Panther). Black, red and blue, necklace in yellow shades. (POL)
136) Poster for a film about partisans (Day of Mopping-up Operations). Black and white with blue bird, red star and olive title. (POL)

130) Plakat für die Aufführung eines deutschen Filmes. (POL)
131) Plakat für einen französischen Film. (POL)
132) Plakat des Volkstheaters für *Elektra* von Richard Strauss. (POL)
133) Plakat für einen Farbfilm (Angelika und der Sultan). (POL)
134) Plakat für die Aufführung der Operette «Das Land des Lächelns» von Franz Lehar. Zwei Grüntöne, weiss und schwarz. (POL)
135) Plakat für eine englische Filmkomödie (Der rosarote Panther). Schwarz, rot und blau, Kollier in gelben Tönen. (POL)
136) Plakat für einen Partisanenfilm (Der Tag der Säuberungs-Aktion). Schwarz und weiss mit blauem Vogel und rotem Stern, Titel in Oliv. (POL)

130) Affiche pour un film allemand. (POL)
131) Affiche pour un film policier français. (POL)
132) Affiche pour une représentation d'*Electre*, de Richard Strauss. (POL)
133) Affiche pour un film en couleur (Angélique et le Sultan). (POL)
134) Affiche pour une opérette de Franz Lehar. Deux tons de vert et noir. (POL)
135) Affiche pour un film anglais (La panthère rose). Noir, rouge et bleu, collier en jaune. (POL)
136) Affiche pour un film sur la résistance. Noir et blanc, oiseau bleu, étoile rouge et titre olive. (POL)

135

134

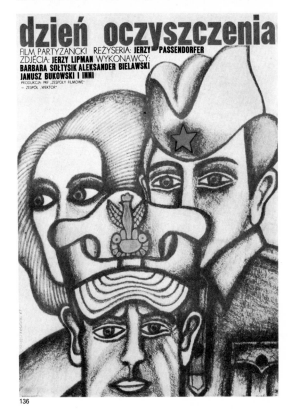

136

Posters / Plakate / Affiches

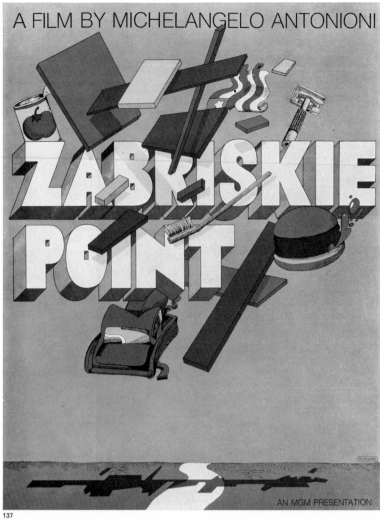

137

138

139

142

137) Polychrome poster for a *Metro-Goldwyn-Mayer* film. (USA)
138) Poster for an opera. Black and white, blue lettering. (GER)
139) Poster for a performance of Chekhov's play *The Three Sisters*. Black and white. (CSR)
140) Poster for a theatre performance of a thriller. Blue-green face, yellow-green ground. (BEL)
141) 'There must be a head.' Poster for a theatre offering a variety of programmes. (GER)
142) Poster for a psychological film. Pastel shades with black. (BUL)
143) Poster for a film (The Big Dig). Polychrome figure. (ISR)
144) Poster for a film (Land of Cockaigne). Title in red and yellow shades on blue ground. (FRA)

Artist | Künstler | Artiste:

137) MILTON GLASER
138) PET HALMEN
139) PAVEL BROM/MILAN KOPRIVA/
     JOSEF KOUDELKA
140) MICHEL WAXMANN
141) JÜRGEN SPOHN
142) ANDRZEJ ONEGIN
143) CYLA MENUSY
144) ANDRÉ FRANÇOIS

Art Director | Directeur artistique:

137) MILTON GLASER
138) DR. GRISCHA BARFUSS
140) MICHEL WAXMANN
141) JÜRGEN SPOHN
142) JERZY WITTEK

Agency | Agentur | Agence – Studio:

137) PUSH PIN STUDIOS, INC., NEW YORK
140) MICHEL WAXMANN, BRUXELLES
141) JÜRGEN SPOHN, BERLIN

---

137) Filmplakat für eine Produktion der *Metro-Goldwyn-Mayer.* (USA)
138) Plakat der Deutschen Oper am Rhein. (GER)
139) Schwarzweisses Plakat für ein Stück von Anton Tschechow, «Die drei Schwestern». Motive nach Chagall. (CSR)
140) Plakat für die Aufführung eines Gruselstückes. Gesicht in blauen und grünen Tönen auf gelbgrünem Grund. (BEL)
141) Mehrfarbiges Theaterplakat mit Hinweis auf die verschiedenen Besucher-Programme der Freien Volksbühne Berlin. (GER)
142) Plakat in Pastellfarben für einen psychologischen Film. (BUL)
143) Plakat für die Aufführung eines Filmes (Das grosse Graben). Mehrfarbige Figur auf weissem Grund. (ISR)
144) Filmplakat (Schlaraffenland). Gelbtöne, Grund blau. (FRA)

137) Affiche polychrome pour un film *Metro-Goldwyn-Mayer.* (USA)
138) Affiche pour un opéra. Noir et blanc, texte en bleu. (GER)
139) Affiche pour une représentation des *Trois soeurs,* de Checkhov. Noir et blanc. (CSR)
140) Affiche pour une pièce d'épouvante au Théâtre des 6 Jetons, Bruxelles. Visage bleu-vert, fond jaune-vert. (BEL)
141) «Il doit bien y avoir une tête.» Affiche pour les programmes d'un théâtre de Berlin. (GER)
142) Affiche pour un film psychologique. Teintes pastels et noir. (BUL)
143) Affiche pour un film. Polychrome sur fond blanc. (ISR)
144) Affiche pour un film de Pierre Etaix. Titre en rouge et jaune sur fond bleu. (FRA)

145

146

147

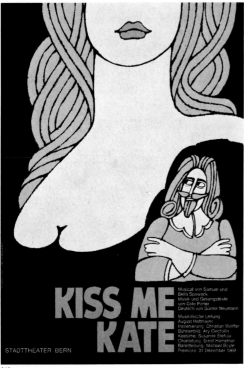

149

150

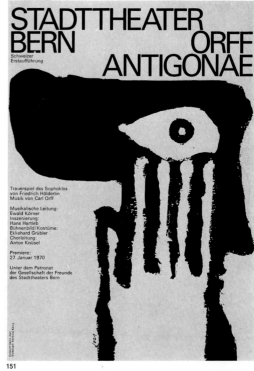

151

145) Poster for a pop film (Pretty Girls, You Mustn't Cry). White figures framed in bright colours. (HUN)
146) Poster for a Russian film with a love-story interest. Polychrome, black lettering. (POL)
147) Poster for a film (The Great Unknown). Black and white with colour accents in eyes, lips and ornaments. (CSR)
148) Poster for a French film comedy. Black and white except for the pink name of Michel Simon. (POL)
149) Poster for a performance of a musical in Berne. Orange, deep pink and black. (SWI)
150) Poster for a performance of a Brecht play in Berne. Black and taupe. (SWI)
151) Poster for a performance of a Greek tragedy with music by Carl Orff. Black and white. (SWI)
152) Poster for a performance of a Lorca tragedy. Black and olive brown. (SWI)
153) Poster for an Italian film (Bandits in Milan). Black and white with red title and sepia bullet-holes. (POL)

145) Plakat für die Aufführung eines Pop-Filmes (Weint nicht, schöne Mädchen). Bunt umrahmte weisse Figuren. (HUN)
146) Plakat für einen russischen Film über eine Liebesgeschichte. Mehrfarbig, schwarze Schrift. (POL)
147) Filmplakat (Die grosse Unbekannte). Schwarzweiss mit farbigen Akzenten in Augen, Lippen und Schmuck. (CSR)
148) Plakat für eine französische Filmkomödie. Schwarzweiss, Namenszug von Michel Simon in Rosa. (POL)
149) Plakat des Stadttheaters Bern für ein Musical. Orange und dunkles Rosa auf Schwarz. (SWI)
150) Theaterplakat. Schwarz und dumpfes Oliv. (SWI)
151) Theaterplakat für eine Erstaufführung. Schwarzweisser Druck auf grau gerastertem Grund. (SWI)
152) Plakat des Stadttheaters Bern für die Aufführung einer tragischen Dichtung von Federico Garcia Lorca. (SWI)
153) Plakat für einen italienischen Film (Banditen in Mailand). Schwarzweiss mit rotem Titel, Schusslöcher schwarz mit Brandspuren in Sepia. (POL)

145) Affiche pour un film «pop» (Ne pleurez pas, jolies filles). Figures blanches encadrées de couleurs vives. (HUN)
146) Affiche pour un film russe racontant une histoire d'amour. Polychrome, texte en noir. (POL)
147) Affiche pour un film (La grande inconnue). Noir et blanc, avec accents de couleur. (CSR)
148) Affiche pour un film français. Noir et blanc, nom de Michel Simon en rose. (POL)
149) Affiche d'un théâtre de Berne, pour une comédie musicale. Orange, rose foncé et noir. (SWI)
150) Affiche pour une représentation d'une pièce de Brecht à Berne. Noir et taupe. (SWI)
151) Affiche pour une représentation d'une tragédie grecque, avec musique de Carl Orff. Noir et blanc. (SWI)
152) Affiche pour une représentation d'une tragédie de Lorca. Noir et brun olive. (SWI)
153) Affiche pour un film italien (Des bandits à Milan). Noir et blanc, titre en rouge, traces de balles en sépia. (POL)

AIR-INDIA

166

162)–165) Posters from a travel series about various regions of France, done for French National Railways by the painter Salvador Dali. (FRA)
166) Poster from a long series for *Air-India*, each referring to a city served by the airline. (IND)
167) Poster for *El Al* Israel Airlines. (ISR)
168) 'Travel without risks...' Poster for French National Railways. Orange car, green bed, blue ground. (FRA)

162)–165) Plakate des Malers Salvador Dali aus einer ganzen Serie der französischen Staatsbahnen über Reiseziele in den verschiedenen Touristikzentren Frankreichs. (FRA)
166) Beispiel aus einer Plakatserie der *Air-India*. Jedes Plakat bezieht sich auf eine Stadt, die von der Fluggesellschaft angeflogen wird. (IND)
167) Plakat der Fluggesellschaft *El Al*. (ISR)
168) «Reisen Sie ohne Gefahr...». Plakat der französischen Staatsbahnen. Fahrzeug in Orange, grünes Bett und blauer Grund. (FRA)

162)–165) Affiches touristiques de Salvador Dali, tirées d'une vaste série de la Société nationale des chemins de fer. (FRA)
166) Affiche tirée d'une série d'*Air-India*, présentant les différentes villes desservies par la compagnie. (IND)
167) Affiche pour la compagnie aérienne israélienne *El Al*. (ISR)
168) Affiche de la Société nationale des chemins de fer. Voiture orange, lit vert, fond bleu. (FRA)

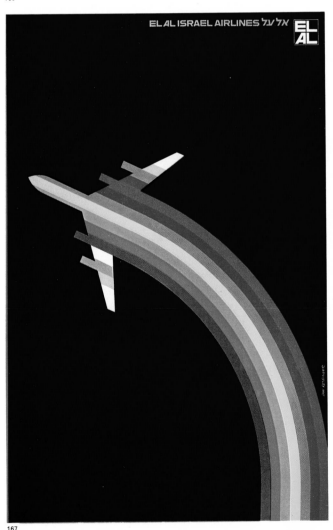

167

168

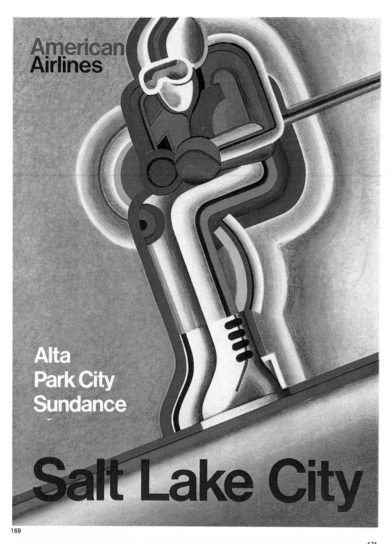

169

170

171

172

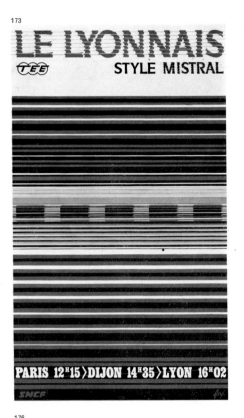

Artist | Künstler | Artiste:

169) PAUL DEGEN
170) 171) GRAHAM CLARKE
172) JOHANN SCHORN
173) FILIPPE FORÉ
174) ATELIER ADE
175) EUGENE HOFFMAN
176) ROGERS/GALBRAITH
177) PAUL KOR
178) JOHN R. RIEBEN

Art Director | Directeur artistique:

169) STEPHAN LION
170) 171) GRAHAM CLARKE
172) JOHANN SCHORN
174) ALBRECHT ADE
175) EUGENE HOFFMAN
176) JIM KERR
177) PAUL KOR
178) JOHN R. RIEBEN

Agency | Agentur | Agence – Studio:

169) DESIGN DYNAMICS, INC., NEW YORK
170) 171) CLARKE/CLEMENTS/HUGHES, MAIDSTONE, KENT/GB
172) MMS, LINZ
173) DEPARTEMENT PUBLICITÉ S.N.C.F., PARIS
174) ATELIER ADE, WUPPERTAL/GER
175) EUGENE HOFFMAN, DENVER
177) DAHAF ADV., TEL-AVIV
178) UNIMARK INTERNATIONAL, DENVER

2

Newspaper Advertisements

Magazine Advertisements

Zeitungs-Inserate

Zeitschriften-Inserate

Annonces de presse

Annonces de revues

Artist | Künstler | Artiste:

179) LAURENCE DREIBAND/JOHN MASSEY
180) VOLKER ANTONI/JOHN MASSEY
181) PINO TOVAGLIA
182) HANS ULRICH OSTERWALDER
183) 184) NORMAN GREEN/WILLIAM WURTZEL

Agency | Agentur | Agence – Studio:

179) 180) N. W. AYER & SON, INC., CHICAGO
182) STUDIO BOGGERI, MILAN
183) 184) THE LAMPERT AGENCY, INC., NEW YORK

Art Director | Directeur artistique:

179) 180) JOHN MASSEY
181) PINO TOVAGLIA
182) ANTONIO BOGGERI
183) 184) WILLIAM WURTZEL

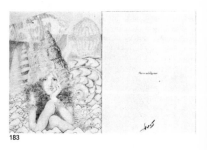

183

179

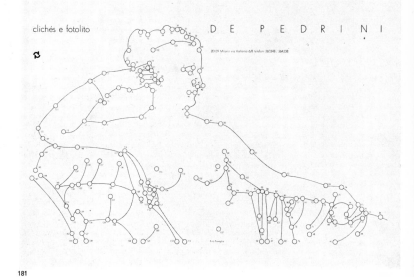

181

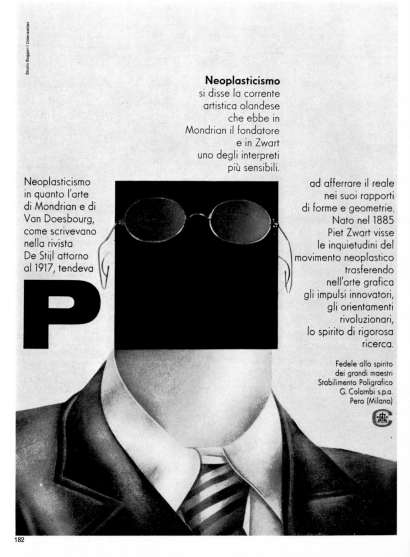

180

182

179) 180) Two double-spread advertisements from the long series for Container Corporation of America in which artists illustrate 'Great Ideas of Western Man'; here quotations from Thomas Carlyle and Albert Einstein. (USA)
181) Advertisement for a photoengraver. (ITA)
182) Magazine advertisement for a photoengraver, referring to Neoplasticism and Piet Zwart. (ITA)
183) 184) Complete advertisement and illustration, for Hanes Hosiery. (USA)

179) 180) Zwei Doppelseiten aus einer langen Serie von Inseraten eines Unternehmens der Verpackungsindustrie, in welchen Künstler «Grosse Gedanken der westlichen Welt» illustrieren, hier Zitate von Thomas Carlyle und Albert Einstein. (USA)
181) Inserat für eine graphische Anstalt. (ITA)
182) Inserat einer graphischen Anstalt, auf Neoplastizismus und Piet Zwart hinweisend. (ITA)
183) 184) Vollständiges Inserat und Illustration für einen Wirkwarenfabrikanten. (USA)

179) 180) Annonces sur doubles pages, tirées d'une longue série pour une entreprise de conditionnement et consacrées aux «Grandes idées de l'homme occidental»; il s'agit ici de citations de Thomas Carlyle et d'Einstein. (USA)
181) Annonce pour l'atelier de photogravure De Pedrini, Milan. (ITA)
182) Annonce pour un atelier de photogravure, G. Colombi S.p.A., Pero. (ITA)
183) 184) Annonce et son illustration, pour la lingerie féminine *Hanes*. (USA)

185

186

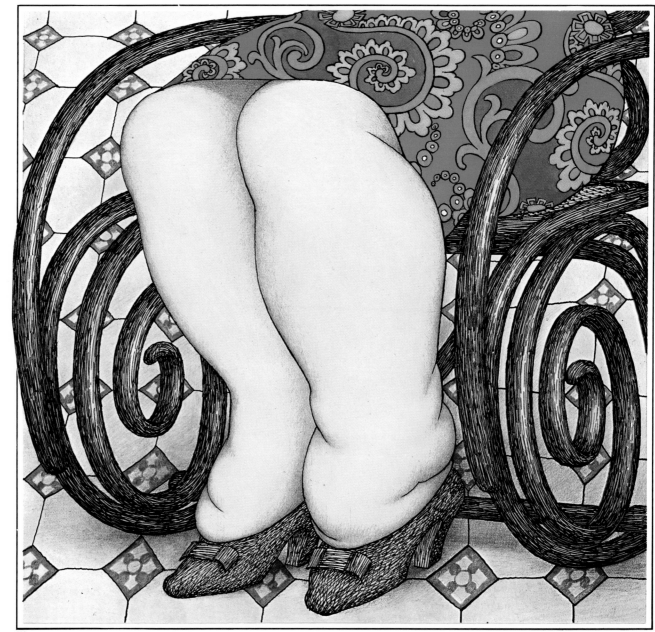

190

Advertisements
Inserate / Annonces

187

188

191

192

185) Double-spread advertisement in full colour for a *Roche* drug to combat the 'paralysing' effects of anxiety. (USA)
186) 187) Full-page newspaper advertisements for synthetic textiles made by Waumbec Mills. Black and white. (USA)
188) Double-spread introductory advertisement for the typographic company Lubalin, Burns & Co. Black and white. (USA)
189) 190) Complete advertisement and corresponding illustration for a new diuretic. (SPA)
191) 192) Page and double spread of a three-page full-colour insert for Broadcast Music, Inc., which specializes in Country music. (USA)

185) Doppelseitiges mehrfarbiges Inserat für ein Medikament gegen die lähmenden Auswirkungen der Angst. (USA)
186) 187) Ganzseitige Zeitungsinserate für synthetische Stoffe eines Textilunternehmens. Schwarzweiss. (USA)
188) Schwarzweisses, doppelseitiges Einführungsinserat für ein typographisches Unternehmen. (USA)
189) 190) Vollständiges Inserat und Illustration für ein neues Diuretikum. (SPA)
191) 192) Seite und Doppelseite eines dreiseitigen, mehrfarbigen Inserates für einen Musikverlag, der sich vorwiegend auf ländliche Musik spezialisiert. (USA)

185) Annonce pour un médicament *Roche* destiné à neutraliser les effets de l'angoisse. Double page en couleur. (USA)
186) 187) Annonces de presse pour des tissus synthétiques. Page entière en noir et blanc. (USA)
188) Annonce sur double page pour un nouvel atelier de typographie. Noir et blanc. (USA)
189) 190) Annonce et son illustration pour une préparation diurétique des Laboratoires Jorba, Madrid. (SPA)
191) 192) Page et double page d'un encart polychrome de trois pages pour un éditeur de musiques, spécialisé dans la musique folklorique. (USA)

The Flour Service looks for trouble before it even turns up.

In the Flour Service, first things always come first.

Long before a new wheat crop is even harvested, our agents are out in the fields. Looking. Tasting. Testing.

By the time the combines go out, our results are in.

So we always have the latest word on what's new in wheat. If tomorrow's flour will need different maturing levels, we know about it beforehand. And exactly how much Maturox it will take to do the job.

We've yet to meet a crop we couldn't handle.

But if you think that we treat all this information as top secret, please don't. It's yours for the asking.

Because in the Flour Service, we're not content just to sell you the right products. We've got to know that you're getting the most out of them.

So, if one of our agents tells you how much Maturox you should be using next year, he's not trying to meddle in your business. He's only taking care of ours.

PENNWALT·
W&T FLOUR SERVICE

Dawn Patrol.

193

ORANGERIE

*Viele Oranges hängen am Baum von GS.
Süße, herbe, schwere, müde, spitze, steile,
grelle, milde, weiche, wilde.
Appetitlich bieten sie sich an.
An jedes ist ranzukommen.
Keine andere Farbe schmeckt so gut...
bei Gebr. Schmidt.*

194

Appetitfarben

Der Hunger kommt von selbst,
der Appetit kommt vom Hinsehen,
das Hinsehen machen die Farben.

Das Auge verschlingt die Farbe.
Das Rosarostbraun eines Steaks.
Butterblumengelbe Spaghettis.
Das gelbockerorangebraune Krustengebirge
eines frischen Brötchens.
Und das Rotweißrot-Gemälde
eines Holsteiner Katenschinkens.

Unsere Zunge schmeckt die Farben,
bevor die Zähne zugebissen haben.

Jedes Menü ist ein Menü der Farben.
Vom Hors d'oeuvre-Rosa eines Lachses
bis zum Tiefbraun-Dessert einer Dame blanche.

Ein Essen ohne Farbe ist ein Essen ohne Duft
und ohne Geschmack.
Im Dunkeln kann man das Essen nicht genießen.

Ein graues Steak ist kein Steak,
eine weiße Tomate keine Tomate.

Schwarz-weiß ist ungenießbar.

Farbe muß auf den Tisch!
Farbe ist der Appetizer.

Gebr. Schmidt servieren eine der größten
Farb-Speisekarten der Welt.
Für alle Farbgourmets und Farbenfeinschmecker.
Die „4 Sterne-Karte" für den Connesseur.

Bon appetit!

Appetitfarben von den Druckfarbenfabriken Gebr. Schmidt GmbH

195

The Flour Service can tell you where your flour went wrong.

Anybody's flour can go astray. Even though they've always given it the best of everything.

The trick is to catch it before the situation gets criminal.

So, the moment you get the feeling that things aren't going right, call The Flour Service. Or better yet, rush a sample to our crime lab in Chicago.

We'll begin interrogation immediately. Putting your flour on the spot. Under the microscope. And in the oven. Round-the-clock, if need be.

We keep after it until we find out what went wrong. And when we do, you're the first (and only) one to know.

Since everything that passes between your mill and The Flour Service is treated as confidential.

Our only concern is that our products, like Maturox and Novadelox, are giving you the kind of flour you expected them to. And if not, then why not.

Nobody's flour puts one over on us.

PENNWALT·
W&T FLOUR SERVICE

We have ways of making flour talk.

198

Artist | Künstler | Artiste:

193) OLAF LEU
194) MILTON GLASER/OLAF LEU
195)–198) GUY BILLOUT

Art Director | Directeur artistique:

193) 194) OLAF LEU
195)–198) T. DA ROLD

Agency | Agentur | Agence – Studio:

193) 194) WEST MEDIA,
       FRANKFURT/M.
195)–198) LORD, GELLER,
       FEDERICO & PARTNERS,
       INC., NEW YORK

193) Double-spread advertisement for printing inks. Orange
     shades on green, white lettering. (GER)
194) Magazine advertisement for 'appetizing' printing inks. Full-
     colour illustration. (GER)
195)–198) Trade press ads and illustration for the Pennwalt Wet
     Flour Service. Black and white. (USA)

193) Doppelseitiges Inserat der Druckfarbenfabrik Gebr.
     Schmidt GmbH., Frankfurt. Abgestufte Töne in Orange
     auf Grün, Schrift weiss. (GER)
194) Mehrfarbiges Inserat der Gebr. Schmidt GmbH. (GER)
195)–198) Fachzeitschrifteninserate und Illustration für ein Mehl-
     untersuchungs-Laboratorium. (USA)

193) Annonce pour des encres d'imprimerie. Tons d'orange sur
     vert, texte en blanc. (GER)
194) Annonce de revue pour des encres d'imprimerie «appé-
     tissantes». Illustration polychrome. (GER)
195)–198) Annonces et illustration pour un laboratoire d'ana-
     lyse de farines. Noir et blanc. (USA)

197

TAKE PRIDE. "THE THREE MUSKETEERS" WAS WRITTEN BY A BLACK MAN. NOW THERE'S AN EXCITING WAY TO LEARN HIS STORY.

The thrilling story of Alexander Dumas is just one of the stories available in The Golden Legacy Series on Negro History. Factual, fun to read magazine stories about the heroics of Crispus Attucks, Patriot, Matthew Henson, Explorer, Benjamin Banneker, Inventor, and others. The Coca-Cola Company offers your children a complete collection of these 32-page adventures. Eleven exciting volumes for just $1.75. Or volume One through Six for only $1.00. Fill your children in on Negro History by filling out the coupon. Sorry, orders for individual volumes cannot be accepted.

ORDER SETS FOR YOUR CHILDREN AND FRIENDS.

It's the real thing. Coke.

199

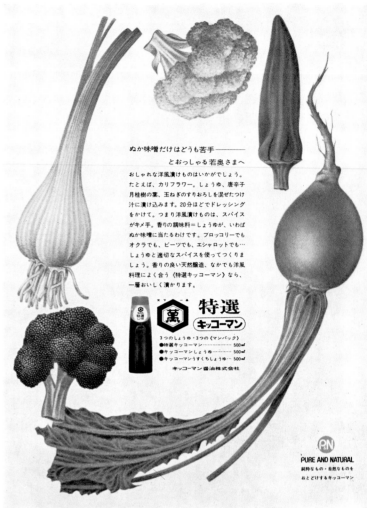

201

New-Hope Soap

Clearasil® Medicated Soap happily announces a new improved formula that means new hope for your troubled skin. New Clearasil Soap has super-sudsing power that really gets down to pores and cleans out dirt and excess oil.

Plus Hexachlorophene to protect you—it fights off the bacteria that can spread blemishes. Use Clearasil Soap anywhere you've got problems...face, neck, shoulders, back—but use it! New sudsier Clearasil Soap—the New-Hope Soap.

200

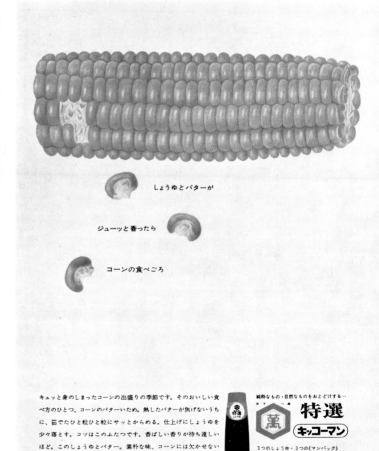

しょうゆとバターが

ジューッと香ったら

コーンの食べごろ

202

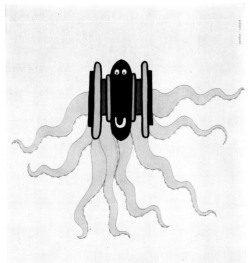

Possente come una piovra

GIUNTOFLEX®

Il nuovo giunto di espansione brevettato
Resiste a sollecitazioni di ogni tipo, alle alte pressioni, alle vibrazioni ed al contatto con vari tipi di fluido. Compensa le dilatazioni e i disassamenti delle tubazioni. La particolare struttura "gomma armatura metallica" costituisce un insieme di eccezionale robustezza, flessibilità e funzionalità.

222

The sun never sets on the Ex-Cell-O weather report.

The U.S. Navy sees to that. Over 4,000 atmospheric reports—from Mandalay to Manhattan—are fed continuously into a central data processing network, built around five of our memory drum systems. The Navy makes about six billion computations from the data, then converts it into the simplified forecasts needed for fleet operations. Fast, foolproof, right-as-rain. Surprised? Well, you probably also didn't know that we help roll strip steel, match piston pins to pistons and ride missiles to the moon. Fancy that. The sun and the moon.

XLO
EX-CELL-O CORPORATION

223

Cellophan ist von KALLE

KALLE

Kalle Aktiengesellschaft, 6202 Wiesbaden-Biebrich, Telefon (06120) 681

224

Formica give you more research than any other laminate maker.

It's true. The FORMICA* laminate you buy has undergone more rigorous testing than any other brand of laminate.

It's been tested for heat resistance, scratch resistance, impact resistance and stain resistance.

But Formica research goes far deeper than that.

It brings you revolutionary new surfaces like FORMICA Suede Finish laminate that holds light, instead of reflecting it. And FORMICA Textured Finish laminate for giving walls a new lease of life.

Formica research means that there's a FORMICA laminate for practically any surfacing job – from exteriors to furniture.

Formica research means that we can actually bend our laminate into the most surprising shapes.

Formica research means you can write to Rodney Rippin at 84 Regent Street, London W1, and ask him to do practically any surfacing job with FORMICA laminate.

FORMICA **The best laminate in the world.**

For details of the new colour range write to Rodney Rippin Formica Limited, 84 Regent Street, London W1   *FORMICA is a registered trade mark. (§) a De La Rue company

225

Alcoa answers the call of the wild with spirited colors and prints.

Change for the better with Alcoa Aluminum

ALCOA

226

83

227

228

229

230

231

232

234

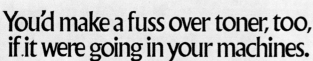

233

227) 228) Page and double spread from an advertisement feature for *Potterton* central heating systems, using three-dimensional models. (GB)
229) Double spread from an insert on *Fiat* vehicles and engines. Orange, pink and blue on green ground. (ITA)
230) Magazine advertisement for a 'packaged' waste disposal system of the Rust Engineering Co. Illustration in full colour. (USA)
231) Magazine advertisement for a *Minolta* camera for close-up work. Insect in colour. (USA)
232) From a series of magazine advertisements for the drum and disc memories of the Vermont Research Corp. Full colour. (USA)
233) Trade advertisement about the toner used in *Xerox* photocopying machines. (USA)
234) Magazine advertisement in full colour conveying Christmas greetings for *Shell*. (ITA)

227) 228) Seite und Doppelseite aus einer Beilage für ein Zentralheizungssystem mit Abbildungen von dreidimensionalen farbigen Hausmodellen. (GB)
229) Doppelseite einer Beilage über Fahrzeuge und Motoren der Marke *Fiat*. Orange, Rosa und Blau auf grünem Grund. (ITA)
230) Inserat für ein vollständiges Kehrichtverbrennungssystem, das so einwandfrei funktioniert, dass keine Luftverschmutzung entsteht und der Himmel «blau» bleibt. (USA)
231) Zeitschrifteninserat für eine *Minolta*-Kamera für Nahaufnahmen. Farbig. (USA)
232) Aus einer Serie mehrfarbiger Inserate für elektronische Speicher. (USA)
233) Inserat für *Xerox*-Photokopiergeräte. (USA)
234) Zeitschrifteninserat mit Glückwünschen zum Jahreswechsel von *Shell*. (ITA)

227) 228) Page et double page d'une rubrique publicitaire pour un système de chauffage central; illustrations polychromes tridimensionnelles. (GB)
229) Double page d'un encart consacré aux moteurs et aux voitures *Fiat*. Orange, rose et bleu sur fond vert. (ITA)
230) Annonce en faveur d'un système d'incinération des ordures, conçu de manière à ne pas polluer l'air environnant. Illustration polychrome. (USA)
231) Annonce de revue pour un appareil photographique *Minolta*. Polychrome. (USA)
232) D'une série d'annonces de revue pour les mémoires d'ordinateurs d'un institut de recherches. Polychrome. (USA)
233) Annonce pour un colorant utilisé dans les machines à polycopier *Xerox*. (USA)
234) Annonce de revue exprimant les bons vœux de la *Shell* italienne. Polychrome. (ITA)

235

Gott schuf die Welt in Farben.

Farbfernseher **BLAUPUNKT**

239

236

237

To horsewhip the peach tree a fine crop does make.

238

The Sub Rosa Subway or **GOLDFISH & BRAHMS** beneath the **GREAT WHITE WAY**

240

235) 236) Illustration and promotional advertisement for a filmed musical version of Dickens' *Christmas Carol* made by Cinema Center Films. Black and white. (USA)

237) 238) 241) Double-spread magazine advertisements from a series for Dow Chemical Co., here relating to soil fumigants, light metals and plastics for furniture. (USA)

239) 240) 'God created the earth in colour.' Advertisement and illustration for a colour television set. (SWI)

235) 236) Illustration und vollständiges Inserat für eine verfilmte Version eines Musicals nach Dickens' *Weihnachtsgeschichten*. Schwarzweiss. (USA)

237) 238) 241) Doppelseitige Beispiele aus einer Inseratenserie für ein Unternehmen der chemischen Industrie, hier für Schädlingsbekämpfung, Leichtmetalle und Plastik für Möbel. Alle drei Inserate mehrfarbig. (USA)

239) 240) Inserat und Illustration für das Farbfernsehgerät *Blaupunkt* der Robert Bosch AG, Zürich. (SWI)

235) 236) Illustration et annonce pour la version filmée d'une comédie musicale tirée des *Contes de Noël* de Charles Dickens. Noir et blanc. (USA)

237) 238) 241) Annonces de revue sur doubles pages, tirées d'une série pour une usine de produits chimiques et se référant, ici, aux pesticides ainsi qu'aux métaux légers et aux matières plastiques pour les meubles. Polychromes. (USA)

239) 240) «Dieu créa la terre en couleur.» Annonce et son illustration pour un téléviseur couleur. (SWI)

The Dow Chemical Company, Plastics Department, Midland, Michigan 48640.

£72/19ˢ/6ᵈ
f.o.b. St. Martins Lane,
London

Please be advised, however, to place order well in advance, like three years or more. The rich-grained red calamander, satinwood and mahogany must be wrested from remote rain forests and tropical islands. Then painstakingly cut, shaped and matched. Then varnished and rubbed, and varnished and rubbed again to a satiny luster before becoming a magnificent escritoire or armoire. All this adds up to years to make one piece—and costs a pretty shilling.

Cabinetry reached its zenith during the 18th century; in the skilled hands of Thomas Chippendale and George Heppelwhite

and their fellow craftsmen. To duplicate their creations today would be prohibitive. Except for materials unknown to these geniuses. New materials that can express the essence of the original—without duplicating its cost, time or labor requirements.

Plastic is such a material. In furniture or whatever, it's often superior to the material it replaces. It has more design flexibility. And there are enough material options to pick exactly the right one.

Plastic is a material that puts no bounds on your capacity to conceive intricate new fantasies. And produce them. And sell them. F.O.B. wherever you want.

 DOW

241

242

243

Advertisements / Inserate / Annonces

242) Magazine advertisement for AT&T to encourage people to telephone birthday greetings. (USA)
243) 244) From a series of magazine advertisements for aluminium foil made by Anaconda Aluminum Co. The full-colour ads are printed on paper laminated with a layer of aluminium foil. (USA)
245) 246) Illustration and complete trade magazine advertisement for blending control equipment made by Singer American Meter Controls. Reprints of the drawing are offered free of charge. (USA)

242) Zeitschrifteninserat einer Telephon- und Telegraphengesellschaft mit der Aufforderung, Geburtstagsglückwünsche auch über grosse Distanzen hinweg telephonisch zu übermitteln. (USA)
243) 244) Aus einer Serie von Zeitschrifteninseraten für Aluminiumfolien. Die Inserate sind auf mit einer Aluminiumfolie kaschiertes Papier gedruckt, wodurch die Farben metallisch leuchten. (USA)
245) 246) Illustration und vollständiges Inserat für Fachzeitschriften, Steuergeräte für Mischapparate anpreisend. Abzüge der Zeichnung werden gratis offeriert. (USA)

242) Annonce de revue d'une compagnie de téléphone et de télégraphe, invitant le public à transmettre ses vœux d'anniversaire par téléphone. (USA)
243) 244) D'une série d'annonces de revue pour la feuille d'aluminium Anaconda. Les couleurs vives sont imprimées sur du papier laminé d'une feuille d'aluminium et prennent ainsi un éclat fluorescent. (USA)
245) 246) Illustration et annonce correspondante de revue professionnelle, en faveur d'appareils de commande pour malaxeurs. On peut obtenir gratuitement des reproductions du dessin. (USA)

244

245

Artist | Künstler | Artiste :

242) FRANK BOZZO

243) 244) ARNOLD VARGA

245) 246) RONALD SEARLE/ANTHONY V. LEONE

Art Director | Directeur artistique :

242) ART TAYLOR

243) 244) JIM MARKLE/TOM LADYGA

245) 246) ANTHONY V. LEONE

Agency | Agentur | Agence – Studio :

242) N.W. AYER & SON, INC., NEW YORK

243) 244) GRISWOLD-ESHLEMAN CO., PITTSBURGH

245) 246) LEWIS & GILMAN, INC., PHILADELPHIA

Advertisements / Inserate / Annonces

247) Magazine advertisement for *Air France*. (FRA)

248) Double-spread magazine advertisement for the 'seven suns' (Miami, Puerto Rico, The Bahamas, Bermuda, Mexico, The Virgin Islands and California) served by Eastern Airlines. (USA)

249) 250) Illustration in colour and complete double-spread magazine advertisement for a sports programme by MGM Television, here referring to the question of brutality in American football. (USA)

251) Magazine advertisement with full-colour illustrations for a holiday touring ticket offered by German Railways. (GER)

252) Double-spread advertisement in colour with a quiz about holiday destinations (mountain, forest or seaside), for German Railways. (GER)

247) Zeitschrifteninserat der Fluglinie *Air France*. (FRA)

248) Doppelseitiges Zeitschrifteninserat für Reisen zu den «sieben Sonnen» (Miami, Puerto Rico, die Bahamas, Bermuda, Mexiko, die Jungferninseln und Kalifornien), die von den Eastern Airlines angeflogen werden. (USA)

249) 250) Farbige Illustration und zweiseitiges Inserat für ein Sportprogramm einer Fernsehgesellschaft, mit Hinweis auf überhandnehmende Brutalität im amerikanischen Fussball. (USA)

251) Zeitschrifteninserat mit mehrfarbigen Illustrationen für ein Ferien-Rundreisebillet der Deutschen Bundesbahnen. (GER)

252) Doppelseitiges Inserat aus einer Kampagne der Deutschen Bundesbahnen zur Förderung des Sommertourismus. Mehrfarbig. (GER)

247) Annonce de revue pour *Air France*. (FRA)

248) Annonce de revue sur double page pour les «sept soleils» (Miami, Porto Rico, les Bahamas, les Bermudes, Mexico, les îles Vierges et la Californie), desservis par la compagnie aérienne Eastern Airlines. (USA)

249) 250) Illustration en couleur et annonce correspondante (double page de revue) pour une émission sportive à la télévision, se référant ici à la brutalité du football américain. (USA)

251) Annonce de revue illustrée en couleur, en faveur d'un abonnement général de vacances des chemins de fer allemands. (GER)

252) Annonce tirée d'une campagne publicitaire des chemins de fer allemands, évoquant les villégiatures d'été (montagne, forêt ou mer). (GER)

247

248

249

251

250

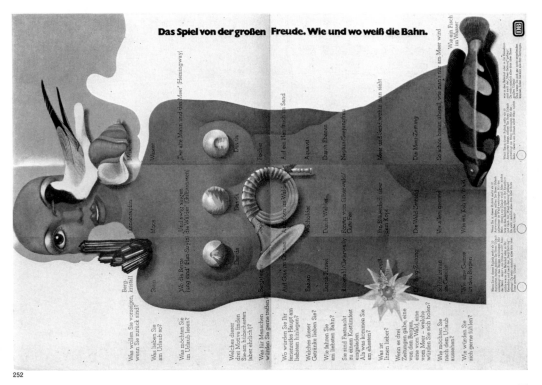

252

253) Space promotion advertisement placed in the trade press by SEVENTEEN magazine. Black and white. (USA)

254) 258) 259) Illustrations (in full colour) and complete double spread from a space promotion series for SPORTS ILLUSTRATED. (USA)

255) Magazine advertisement with colour illustration for the CNA insurance company, offering corporations attractive fringe benefit schemes. (USA)

256) 257) Space promotion advertisements placed in magazines by SPORTS ILLUSTRATED. Fig. 256 is addressed to car manufacturers. (USA)

253) Anzeige einer Zeitschrift in der Fachpresse zur Werbung von Inserenten für die eigenen Spalten. Schwarzweiss. (USA)

254) 258) 259) Mehrfarbige Illustrationen und vollständige, doppelseitige Anzeige aus einer Serie zur Werbung von Inserenten für ein illustriertes Sportmagazin. (USA)

255) Zeitschrifteninserat mit farbiger Illustration für eine Versicherungsgesellschaft, die der Geschäftswelt Versicherungen mit attraktiven Nebenleistungen als Teil einer erfolgreichen Personalpolitik empfiehlt. (USA)

256) 257) Anzeigen eines Sportmagazins in Zeitschriften zur Inserentenwerbung für die eigene Publikation. Abb. 256 wendet sich an die Herstellerfirmen der Automobilbranche. (USA)

253) Annonce de revue professionnelle pour la publicité dans le magazine SEVENTEEN. Noir et blanc. (USA)

254) 258) 259) Illustrations polychromes et une des annonces correspondantes sur double page, tirées d'une série pour une revue sportive. (USA)

255) Annonce de revue d'une compagnie d'assurance, suggérant aux grandes entreprises d'intéressants plans de participation aux bénéfices pour leurs employés. Illustration en couleur. (USA)

256) 257) Annonce de revue pour la publicité dans un magazine sportif. L'ill. 256 s'adresse aux fabricants d'automobiles. (USA)

253

256

257

254

In 1939 it didn't take much talent to make a corporation look good to employees.
A dull name on a dull check was attractive.
But this is 1970. When American corporations' most attractive features are hidden incomes: the fringes.
And making employee benefit fringes attractive takes talent.
Paid holidays, paid vacations, Group Hospital Insurance and Group Life Insurance don't dazzle anyone today. They're expected.
If a corporation wants its hidden incomes to dazzle, they had better look more like this:

24-hour Accidental Death; Long Term Disability; Non-Contributory Group Life. Policies that have been standards with us for years.
We're CNA. And we're constantly working on new fringes for companies. Fringes that an employer contributes to only if he chooses.
Payroll Deductible Fringes.
Attractive employee benefits that cost your corporation little or nothing.
CNA has even developed programs like

Auto and Homeowners for your employees. And we'll continue to develop more. Lots more.
Contact your agent. Or write to us.
Talk to us about your hidden incomes.
For practically nothing, we'll help make you attractive to your most important asset. Your people.

Announcing fringe benefits that make a company look good.

Have it your way.
⸭CNA/insurance

255

258

259

Artist / Künstler / Artiste:

253) RICHARD STEWART
254) THOMAS B. ALLEN/RONALD DEMILT
255) EDWARD SOREL
256) ANDRÉ FRANÇOIS/RONALD DEMILT
257) BLAKE HAMPTON/BOB CZERNYSZ
258) 259) PAUL DAVIS/RONALD DEMILT

Art Director / Directeur artistique:

253) RICHARD STEWART
254) 256) 258) 259) RICHARD GANGEL/BOB CZERNYSZ
255) BUD WATTS
257) BOB CZERNYSZ

Agency / Agentur / Agence – Studio:

253) SEVENTEEN MAGAZINE, PROMOTION ART
    DEPARTMENT, NEW YORK
254) 256)–259) YOUNG & RUBICAM, INC., NEW YORK
255) POST, KEYES, GARDNER, INC., CHICAGO

260) Magazine advertisement for *Talon* zip fasteners. (USA)
261) 'Don't sell incognito.' Advertisement for *De Beers* diamonds. (FRA)
262) Magazine advertisement for *Coca-Cola*. (USA)
263) Advertisement for a new boutique in Bienne. (SWI)
264) Magazine advertisement in full colour for *Talon* zip fasteners. (USA)
265) Magazine advertisement for a deodorant with the scent of 'Japanese gardens'. Full colour. (FRA)
266) Newspaper advertisement for a maker of packaging machines. (SWI)
267) From a series of advertisements for a furrier. Full colour. (ITA)

Artist / Künstler / Artiste:

260) PAUL DAVIS/PAUL JERVIS
261) JEAN FORTIN
262) JOHN ALCORN/AL SCULLY
263) ARMIN GREDER
264) ETIENNE DELESSERT
265) ALAIN LEFOLL
266) HANS-GEORG RAUCH
267) ILIO NEGRI

Art Director / Directeur artistique:

260) PAUL JERVIS
261) JEAN FORTIN
262) AL SCULLY
263) ARMIN GREDER
264) LARRY OSBORNE
265) DANIEL BOUR
266) PETER SCHOLL
267) ILIO NEGRI

Agency / Agentur / Agence – Studio:

260) 264) DKG, INC., NEW YORK
261) 265) PUBLICIS CONSEIL, PARIS
262) McCANN-ERICKSON, INC., NEW YORK
263) ATELIER DU CYCLOPE, BIEL/SWI
266) WERBEAGENTUR ALEXANDRE OTT, ZÜRICH
267) STUDIO NEGRI, MILAN

260

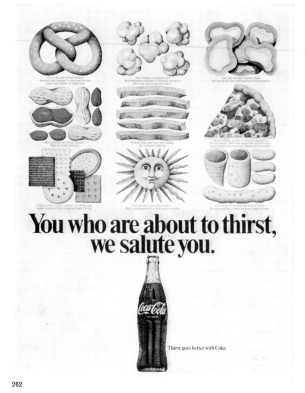

262

261

263

260) «Diesen Schrei der Wildnis verdanken Sie einem beschädigten Reissverschluss». Inserat für *Talon*-Reissverschlüsse. (USA)
261) «Verkaufen Sie nicht inkognito». Für *De Beers*-Diamanten. (FRA)
262) Zeitschrifteninserat für *Coca-Cola*. (USA)
263) Inserat für das neue Modegeschäft «New Shop» in Biel. (SWI)
264) Zeitschrifteninserat, mehrfarbig, für *Talon*-Reissverschlüsse. (USA)
265) Für einen Deodorant, der nach «japanischen Gärten» duftet. (FRA)
266) Zeitungsinserat für die SIG, Schweizerische Industriegesellschaft in Neuhausen, für die Abteilung Verpackungsmaschinen. (SWI)
267) Aus einer Inseratenserie für einen Kürschner. Mehrfarbig. (ITA)

260) Annonce de revue pour les fermetures à glissière *Talon*. (USA)
261) Annonce en faveur des diamants *De Beers*. (FRA)
262) Annonce de revue pour le *Coca-Cola*. (USA)
263) Annonce pour une nouvelle boutique de mode à Bienne. (SWI)
264) Annonce polychrome pour les fermetures à glissière *Talon*. (USA)
265) Annonce de revue pour le dédorant O.BA.O. dont le parfum rappelle un «jardin japonais». (FRA)
266) Annonce pour un fabricant de machines de conditionnement. (SWI)
267) Annonce en couleur d'une série pour le pelletier Ciwipel, Milan. (ITA)

SINCE WINTER IS RIGHT AROUND THE CORNER, WE'D LIKE TO REMIND YOU WHAT A BROKEN JACKET ZIPPER FEELS LIKE.

What better time to point out the faults of some zippers and the virtues of ours than in September. Before you buy a jacket that leaves you out in the cold, cold.

SEPTEMBER 20, 1970

in the cold, cold.

The Talon Zephyr® nylon jacket zipper is designed not to snag, grab, jam, or break in the middle of a December blizzard.

Or an April shower.

The Talon Zephyr zipper will go up when you want it to go up, and down when you want it to go down. So make sure our

zipper is in your jacket.

That way if you come down with a cold this winter, the only thing you'll be able to blame it on is the weather.

Talon
THE QUALITY NYLON ZIPPER
DIVISION OF TEXTRON

264

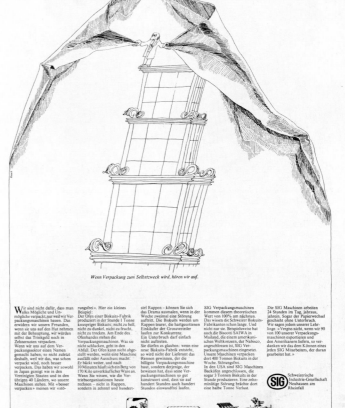

Wenn Verpackung zum Selbstzweck wird, hören wir auf.

Wir sind nicht dafür, dass man alles Mögliche verpackt, nur weil wir Verpackungsmaschinen bauen. Das erwidern wir unsern Freunden, wenn sie uns auf den Hut nehmen mit der Behauptung, wir würden selbst das Trinkgeld noch in Zehnernoten verpacken. Wenn wir uns auf dem Verpackungssektor einen Namen gemacht haben, so nicht zuletzt deshalb, weil wir das, was schon verpackt wird, noch besser verpacken. Das haben wir sowohl in Japan gezeigt wie in den Vereinigten Staaten und in den übrigen 40 Ländern, wo unsere Maschinen stehen. Mit «besser verpacken» meinen wir «stö-

rungsfrei». Hier ein kleines Beispiel: Der Ofen einer Biskuits-Fabrik produziert in der Stunde 1 Tonne knuspriger Biskuits; nicht zu hell, nicht zu dunkel, nicht zu feucht, nicht zu trocken. Am Ende des Ofenbandes stehen die Verpackungsmaschinen. Was sie nicht schlucken, geht in den Abfall. Der Ofen kann nicht abgestellt werden, wenn eine Maschine ausfällt oder Ausschuss macht. Er blickt weiter, und nach 10 Minuten häuft sich ein Berg von 170 Kilos unverkäuflicher Ware an. Wenn Sie wissen, wie die Verpackungsorganisationen heute rechnen – nicht in Rappen, sondern in zehntel und hundert-

stel Rappen – können Sie sich das Drama ausmalen, wenn in der Woche zweimal eine Störung auftritt. Die Biskuits werden um Rappen teurer, die Hartgesottenen Einkäufer der Grossverteiler laufen zur Konkurrenz. Ein Unterbruch darf einfach nicht auftreten. Sie dürfen es glauben: wenn eine neue Biskuits-Fabrik entsteht, so wird nicht der Lieferant das Rennen gewinnen, der die billigste Verpackungsmaschine baut, sondern derjenige, der bewiesen hat, dass seine Verpackungsmaschinen so gut konstruiert sind, dass sie auf hundert Stunden auch hundert Stunden einwandfrei laufen.

SIG Verpackungsmaschinen kommen diesem theoretischen Wert von 100% am nächsten. Das wissen die Schweizer Biskuits-Fabrikanten schon lange. Und nicht nur sie. Beispielsweise hat auch die Biscotti SAIWA in Mailand, zu einem amerikanischen Weltkonzern, der Nabisco, angeschlossen ist, SIG Verpackungsmaschinen eingesetzt. Unsere Maschinen verpacken dort 400 Tonnen Biskuits in der Woche. Störungsfrei. In den USA sind SIG Maschinen Backöfen angeschlossen, die sogar 3 Tonnen Biskuits in der Stunde produzieren. Eine zehnminütige Störung brächte dort eine halbe Tonne Verlust.

Die SIG Maschinen arbeiten 24 Stunden im Tag, jahraus, jahrein. Sogar der Papierwechsel geschieht ohne Unterbruch. Wir wagen jedem unserer Lehrlinge. «Vergiss nicht, wenn wir 90 von 100 unserer Verpackungsmaschinen exportieren und den Amerikanern liefern, so verdanken wir das dem Können eines jeden SIG Mitarbeiters, der daran gearbeitet hat.»

SIG Schweizerische
Industrie-Gesellschaft
Neuhausen am
Rheinfall

266

**nouveau
le déodorant
après bain
O.BA.O**

Après le bain,
le déodorant O.BA.O
supprime pour toute la journée
les odeurs de transpiration
et prolonge la fraîcheur.
C'est un souffle parfumé
de mousses et de fleurs rares,
un bouquet aux senteurs
des jardins japonais.

OBA.O
DÉODORANT
ATOMISEUR
PROLONGE LA FRAÎCHEUR

OBA.O
L'ART DU BAIN

265

CIWIPEL
20123 MILANO VIA FIENO 3 TEL 864009

COMM. ALFREDO GIAMMETTI 00152 ROMA VIA BASILIO BRICCI 14 TEL. 5039376
RAPPRESENTANTI: RAG. GASTONE MALTAGLIATI 50123 FIRENZE VIA VIGNA NUOVA 3 TEL. 23817
DOTT. MICHELANGELO MORLICCHIO 80121 NAPOLI VIA S. PASQUALE A CHIAIA 30 TEL. 393867
GALLIANO ROMANELLI 10121 TORINO VIA MONTE DI PIETÀ 2 TEL. 519746

267

95

268) Magazine advertisement for Superior Tube, one sixth of whose employees work on quality control. Full-colour illustration. (USA)
269) 270) Illustration and complete double-spread magazine advertisement to encourage football-season advertising in SPORTS ILLUSTRATED. (USA)
271) 272) 'Destroy the horrible smell of cold tobacco.' – 'Destroy the foul smell of the refuse bin.' Black-and-white illustrations from double-spread advertisements used in a campaign for *Air-Wick* air sprays. (FRA)
273) Space promotion advertisement for the magazine SPORTS ILLUSTRATED. (USA)

268) Zeitschrifteninserat für einen Fabrikanten von Rohrleitungen, der einen Sechstel seines Personals für Qualitätskontrollen eingesetzt hat. (USA)
269) 270) Illustration und vollständiges, doppelseitiges Zeitschrifteninserat, das für Inserate in einem Sportmagazin während der Fussball-Saison wirbt. (USA)
271) 272) «Beseitigen Sie den schrecklichen Geruch kalten Tabaks» – «Beseitigen Sie den faulen Kehrichteimer-Geruch». Illustrationen in Schwarzweiss zu zwei doppelseitigen Inseraten aus einer Kampagne für den Luftverbesserungs-Spray *Air-Wick*. (FRA)
273) Anzeige zur Werbung von Inserenten für die Zeitschrift SPORTS ILLUSTRATED (USA)

268) Annonce de revue pour un fabricant de tuyauterie, dont un sixième du personnel est employé au contrôle de la qualité. Illustration en couleur. (USA)
269) 270) Illustration et annonce correspondante sur double page, pour la publicité dans une revue sportive pendant la saison du football. (USA)
271) 272) Illustrations en noir et blanc d'annonces sur doubles pages, parues dans le cadre d'une campagne en faveur de l'épurateur d'air *Air-Wick*. (FRA)
273) Annonce pour la publicité dans un magazine sportif. (USA)

One sixth of our people work in quality assurance. When you insist on the big name in small tubing, you know it will be right on specs. Write for article reprint on testing procedures. (ST) Superior Tube

Norristown, Pa. 19404 West Coast: Pacific Tube Company, Los Angeles, Calif. 90022

268

Détruisez l'horrible odeur du tabac froid.

Détruisez l'infecte odeur de poubelle.

271   272

269

270

We add reach. Where you want it.

Every week, Sports Illustrated reaches some 9 million adults. Which, if the truth be told, is less than some media reach every night.
But what's more important than how many you reach is whom you reach.
While our readers make up a modest 5% of the country's population, they're some 28% of the management men earning $15,000 and up per year.
24% of all men who graduated from college. And 27% of the country's $25,000-a-year men.

(Not bad when you consider that 9 out of 10 men who read SI are under 50.)
And if your product isn't as widely distributed as our audience, we have ten regional and metro editions. Giving you a chance to get our readers exactly where you want them.

Sports Illustrated
The magazine for all seasons.

273

Artist | Künstler | Artiste:

268) SAUL MANDEL
269) 270) MILTON GLASER/RONALD DEMILT
271) 272) MICHEL GUIRÉ-VAKA
273) JEROME MARTIN/RONALD DEMILT

Art Director | Directeur artistique:

268) ELMER PIZZI
269) 270) 273) RICHARD GANGEL/BOB CZERNYSZ
271) 272) JEAN MARIE LEYDIER

Agency | Agentur | Agence – Studio:

268) GRAY & ROGERS, INC., PHILADELPHIA
269) 270) 273) YOUNG & RUBICAM, INC., N.Y.
271) 272) LORIN-LEYDIER, PARIS

274

276

275

The Littlest Elf.

NATIONAL CENTRAL

Artist / Künstler / Artiste:

274) 275) JACKIE GEYER/FRED ROBINSON
276) GERRY GERSTEN/MURRAY SMITH
277) DONNA BROWN/DENNIS GODDARD
278) RENÉ FEHR/ROBERT HÖSLI
279)–281) LARRY SONS

Art Director / Directeur artistique:

274) 275) FRED ROBINSON
276) MURRAY SMITH
277) PETER KROHN
278) RUEDI KÜLLING
279)–281) LARRY SONS

Agency / Agentur / Agence – Studio:

274) 275) KETCHUM, MCLEOD & GROVE, INC., PITTSBURGH
276) DANIEL & CHARLES, INC., NEW YORK
277) KROHN & COMPANY, MONTREAL
278) ADVICO-DELPIRE AG, ZÜRICH
279)–281) STAN RICHARDS & ASSOC., DALLAS

Old Town is Laurel & Hardy and

The Great White Whale, "Open Sesame," a safe landing, and the biggest piece.

It's an Academy Award, half price, three wishes, and live and in color.

Old Town is lots of things. Wonderful things.

It's a beautiful bouquet of trees and flowers surrounding more than 45 unique shops and restaurants.

Old Town is the shopping Mall that's a garden and the garden that's a shopping mall.

Old Town in The Village

Somewhere over the rainbow at Greenville and Lovers Lane

279

274) 275) Illustration und vollständiges Zeitungsinserat für den Weihnachts-
Club eines Bankunternehmens. (USA)
276) Anzeige für die Werbung von Inserenten für ein Sportmagazin. (USA)
277) Zeitungsinserat für Schuhe und Accessoires. (CAN)
278) Inserat für die Schweizerische Bankgesellschaft. (SWI)
279)–281) Aus einer Serie von Kleininseraten für ein Einkaufszentrum. (USA)

274) 275) Illustration et annonce de presse correspondante, en faveur d'un
compte d'épargne pour les achats de Noël. (USA)
276) Annonce pour la publicité dans la revue SPORT. (USA)
277) Annonce de presse pour les chaussures et les accessoires Mayfair. (CAN)
278) Annonce tirée d'une série pour l'Union de Banques Suisses. (SWI)
279)–281) Trois petites annonces pour un centre d'achat de Dallas. (USA)

277

278

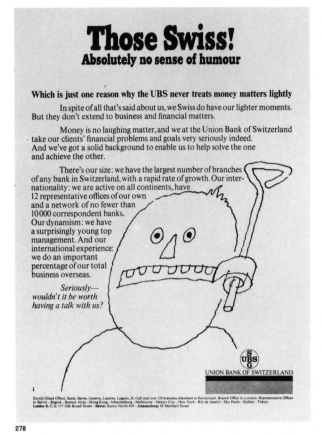

280

281

99

282) 283) Full-page four-colour newspaper advertisements from a series for *Manners* restaurants, here about a new sweet and about their chicken dinners. (USA)

284) Full-page newspaper advertisement for a department store launching a campaign for the products of Israel. (SWI)

285) Newspaper advertisement for *Encron* polyester for city clothing. (USA)

286) Newspaper advertisement for a cement company wishing to open a quarry in a tourist area of the Ticino. (SWI)

287) Full-page newspaper advertisement about the decentralized supply and service system of the *Marcor* packaging group. (USA)

288) Full-page trade newspaper ad for *Waumbec* fire-resisting fabrics. (USA)

289) Space promotion ad for the book review section of THE NEW YORK TIMES. (USA)

282) 283) Ganzseitige Zeitungsinserate einer Serie für die *Manners*-Restaurants, hier für Kuchen und «Poulet-Essen». (USA)

284) Ganzseitiges Zeitungsinserat für das Warenhaus *Loeb* anlässlich einer Kampagne für Produkte aus Israel. (SWI)

285) Zeitungsinserat für Polyester-Stoffe für «städtesichere» Kleidung. (USA)

286) Für einen Zementfabrikanten, der um positive Einstellung zur Eröffnung eines Steinbruches im Tessin wirbt. (SWI)

287) Ganzseitiges Zeitungsinserat über die dezentralisierte Verkaufs- und Service-Organisation einer Gruppe der Verpackungs-Industrie. (USA)

288) Ganzseitiges Fachzeitschrifteninserat für feuersichere Stoffe. (USA)

289) Werbeinserat für den Buchbesprechungsteil einer New Yorker Zeitung. (USA)

282) 283) Annonces de presse tirées d'une série pour une chaîne de restaurants. Doubles pages en couleur. (USA)

284) Annonce de presse d'un grand magasin lançant une campagne en faveur de produits importés d'Israël. (SWI)

285) Annonce de presse en faveur des tissus de polyester *Encron* pour les vêtements de ville. (USA)

286) Annonce de presse en faveur d'une fabrique de ciment, désireuse d'exploiter une carrière dans une région touristique du Tessin. (SWI)

287) Annonce de presse d'une entreprise de conditionnement, en faveur d'un système décentralisé de vente. (USA)

288) Annonce parue dans la presse professionnelle, pour des tissus ininflammables. (USA)

289) Annonce pour la publicité dans le supplément littéraire du NEW YORK TIMES. (USA)

Advertisements
Inserate / Annonces

282

284

283

285

Agency | Agentur | Agence – Studio:

282) STUDIO GRAFICO ROMANO CHICHERIO, LUGANO
283) N.W. AYER & SON, INC., CHICAGO
284) KURT WIRTH, BERN
285) DKG, INC., NEW YORK
286) 287) WYSE ADVERTISING, INC., CLEVELAND
288) DON WISE & CO., INC., NEW YORK
289) THE NEW YORK TIMES, PROMOTION DEPT., NEW YORK

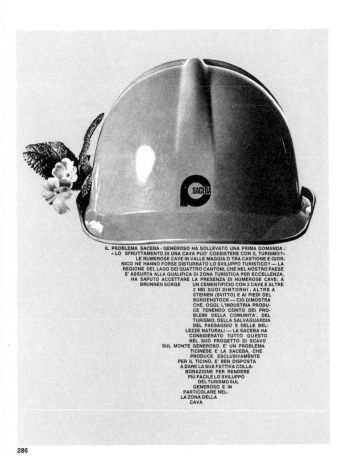

286

287

288

The drapery salesman who didn't know any better

289

The Pittsburgh National Christmas Club
makes some of our customers pretty smug
this time of year.

Right now, when everyone else is just beginning to worry
about Christmas, Pittsburgh National Christmas Clubbers
earned the right to be a little smug. Their Christmas Club
accounts are already full.
Pittsburgh National gives away five bayberry candles
just for joining. And a few dollars every other week means
the end to last-minute scraping and after-Christmas
payments that stretch into the better part of next year.
Join the Pittsburgh National Christmas Club and
brighten this year's Christmas with bayberry candles. Next
year's Christmas will take care of itself.

PITTSBURGH NATIONAL
Member Federal Deposit Insurance Corporation
Each depositor insured to $20,000

290

291

We know, we know.
Just about the time you
got really comfortable
with the old Cox's,
we changed it.
There should be a
hall of fame for fine
old shoes, retired after
their millionth footstep.
For thirty year old radios
with tubes that glow orange
in the back. For venerable overstuffed chairs
that sag where father bulges and bulge where father sags.
For lifelong sewing machines, frazzled favorite books,
ancient, unstoppable clocks, paunchy old purses that were
stitched together not long after they invented money,
and stores so familiar you know where the floor boards creak.
Old friends are best—until you want a more stylish shoe,
FM on the radio, zig-zag stitches for your sewing,
or a purse to match your new hat. Or a store
that has all the good old things plus some new ones,
in brighter, more cheerful, more enjoyable surroundings.
It's like a new book by an old favorite author.
Get the best of both worlds. Come in and enjoy the new
Cox's. Then—when nobody is looking—get used to it.

292

I like you just the way you are.

Jog if you want to.
Ride bicycles that don't go anywhere.
Eat watercress, if it makes you happy.
But don't change for me.
The suit is supposed to fit you: why should you change shape
to fit the suit? Or pants, or coat. What am I, lazy?
Why when I get through fitting, the suit will look so good
everyone will want to be your weight.
Why did I apprentice all those years if not for that?
Why else would Horne's have all those good seamstresses
to fit the girls? So you're not a common size.
So what? We're not a common store.
Now, bathing suits? That's different. Joseph Horne Co.

293

294

Artist / Künstler / Artiste:

290) JACKIE GEYER/FRED ROBINSON
291)–295) ARNOLD VARGA

Art Director / Directeur artistique:

290) FRED ROBINSON
291)–295) ARNOLD VARGA

Agency / Agentur / Agence – Studio:

290) KETCHUM, MCLEOD & GROVE, INC.,
PITTSBURGH

290) Full-page four-colour newspaper advertisement for a Christmas club run by the Pittsburgh National Bank. (USA)
291) 293) Full-page newspaper advertisements for the department stores of Joseph Horne Co., here for stationery and men's suits. (USA)
292) Full-page newspaper advertisement for *Cox's* department stores. (USA)
294) 295) Full-page newspaper advertisement and illustration, for avant-garde clothing from the *John Wanamaker* department stores. (USA)

290) Ganzseitiges Zeitungsinserat in vier Farben für einen von einer Bank betriebenen Weihnachts-Club. (USA)
291) 293) Ganzseitige Zeitungsinserate für die Warenhäuser der Joseph Horne & Co., hier für Papeteriewaren und Herrenanzüge. (USA)
292) Ganzseitiges Zeitungsinserat für eine Warenhauskette. (USA)
294) 295) Ganzseitiges Zeitungsinserat und Illustration für die Warenhauskette *John Wanamaker*, hier für neuzeitliche Bekleidung. (USA)

290) Annonce de presse en faveur d'un compte d'épargne pour les achats de Noël. Page entière en quatre couleurs. (USA)
291) 293) Annonces de presse pour les articles de papeterie et les vêtements d'hommes en vente dans un grand magasin. (USA)
292) Annonce de presse sur page entière, pour un grand magasin. (USA)
294) 295) Annonce de presse sur page entière et son illustration, en faveur de vêtements «d'avant-garde» pour messieurs. (USA)

295

296) Full-page newspaper advertisement for a week of night sales in the *Wanamaker* department stores. (USA)

297) 298) Full-page newspaper advertisements for a department store, The May Co., here for exotic scent sprays and a new shirt style. (USA)

299) 300) Full-page newspaper advertisements from a series for Southern Methodist University, intended to encourage private donations to educational institutions. Black and white. (USA)

301) 302) Newspaper advertisements from a series for *Volkswagen* cars, making use of the familiar outline. Black and white. (BEL)

296) Ganzseitiges Zeitungsinserat für die Abendverkäufe eines Warenhauses. (USA)

297) 298) Ganzseitige Zeitungsinserate für ein Warenhaus, hier für Sprays mit exotischen Parfums und für Hemden in einem neuen Stil. (USA)

299) 300) Ganzseitige Zeitungsinserate aus einer Serie für eine Universität, die die Öffentlichkeit zur Unterstützung von Erziehungsinstituten anregt. (USA)

301) 302) Schwarzweisse Zeitungsinserate aus einer Serie von vier für den *Volkswagen*. Die bekannte «Käfer-Linie» wird in zeichnerischer Form ausgewertet. (BEL)

296) Annonce de presse sur page entière pour une semaine de ventes spéciales, le soir, dans les grands magasins *John Wanamaker*. (USA)

297) 298) Annonce de presse sur page entière, pour les parfums exotiques en aérosol et les chemises nouveau style en vente dans un grand magasin. (USA)

299) 300) Annonces de presse, tirées d'une série pour une université méthodiste et destinées à encourager les dons des particuliers aux établissements d'enseignement. Pages entières en noir et blanc. (USA)

301) 302) Annonces de presse tirées d'une série en faveur des voitures *Volkswagen* et interprétant le thème des lignes familières de la «coccinelle». Noir et blanc. (BEL)

297

296

298

299

300

Artist | Künstler | Artiste:

296) DENNIS JOHNSON/CAROL TABACK
297) KIRBY EVANS/ROYSTON & LYNNE EVANS
298) ROYSTON & LYNNE EVANS
299) 300) THE SKETCH PAD/DIANA GILMORE
301) 302) WILLY VAN CLUYSEN/ FRANZ JACOB

Art Director | Directeur artistique:

296) J. MICHAEL DAVISON
297) 298) ROYSTON & LYNNE EVANS
299) 300) DIANA GILMORE
301) 302) WILLY VAN CLUYSEN

Agency | Agentur | Agence – Studio:

297) 298) THE LOVING COUPLE STUDIO, SANTA MONICA
299) 300) BLOOM ADVERTISING AGENCY, INC., DALLAS
301) 302) ROLAND BUSSELEN PUBL., BRUXELLES

301

302

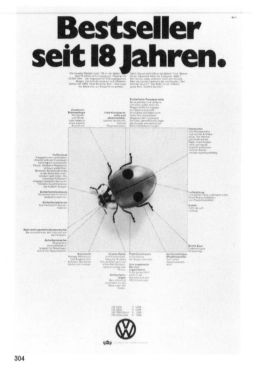

303

304

305

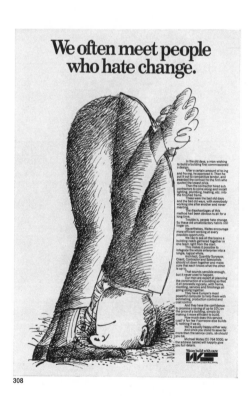

307

308

303) Trade press advertisement for a photoengraver. (SWI)
304) 'Best-seller for 18 years.' Newspaper advertisement for the *Volkswagen*. Black and white. (SWI)
305) Newspaper advertisement for *American Express* tours of Europe. Black and white. (USA)
306) 309) 310) Illustrations and full-page newspaper advertisement for space promotion in the magazine Look. (USA)
307) 308) From a series of advertisements for *Wates* directed against old habits and prejudices in the building trade. (GB)

303) Fachzeitschriften-Inserat der Cliché-Anstalt Denz, Bern. (SWI)
304) Inserat der Amag, Schinznach-Bad, für den *Volkswagen*. (SWI)
305) Inserat eines Reisebüros für Europa-Touren. Schwarzweiss. (USA)
306) 309) 310) Illustrationen und ganzseitiges Zeitungsinserat zur Inserentenwerbung für eine Zeitschrift. (USA)
307) 308) Schwarzweisse Inserate aus einer Kampagne, die von einem fortschrittlichen Bauunternehmen lanciert wurde: «Wir kommen oft mit Leuten zusammen, die jede Änderung hassen» – «*Wates* schlachtet manchmal heilige Kühe». (GB)

303) Annonce de revue professionnelle, pour un photograveur. (SWI)
304) «*Best-seller* depuis 18 ans!» Annonce de presse pour les voitures *Volkswagen*. Noir et blanc. (SWI)
305) Annonce de presse pour une agence de voyages. (USA)
306) 309) 310) Illustrations et annonce de presse sur page entière, pour la publicité dans la revue Look. (USA)
307) 308) D'une série d'annonces lancées par une entreprise du bâtiment et dirigées contre les vieilles habitudes et les idées préconçues en matière de construction. (GB)

Artist / Künstler / Artiste:
303) KURT WIRTH
304) HEINI SUESS
305) 306) TOMI UNGERER/AL ZERRIES
307) DAVID NEWTON
308) DAVID ENGLISH
309) 310) TOMI UNGERER

Art Director / Directeur artistique:
303) KURT WIRTH
304) DOMINIK L. BURCKHARDT
305) 306) AL ZERRIES
307) DAVID NEWTON
308) DAVID ENGLISH

Agency / Agentur / Agence – Studio:
303) KURT WIRTH, BERN
304) WERBEAGENTUR HANS LOOSER, ZÜRICH
305) 306) OGILVY & MATHER, INC., NEW YORK
307) 308) DAVIDSON, PEARCE, BERRY & TUCK LTD., LONDON

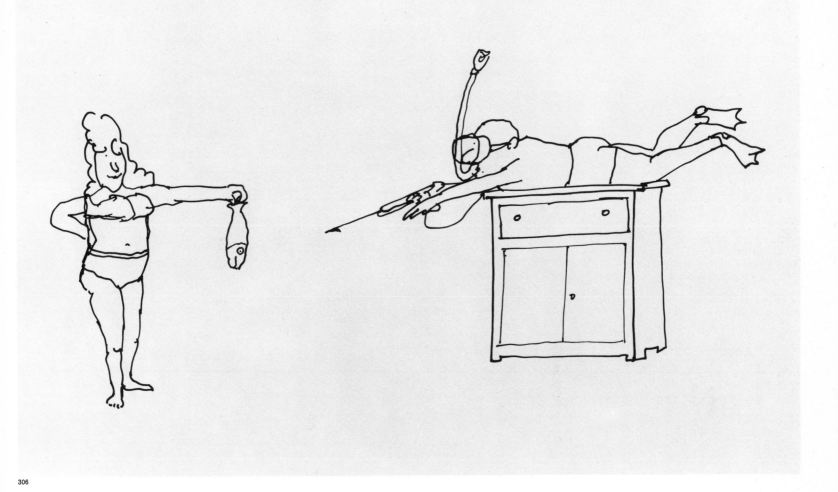

306

Give your kids a head start. Let someone else raise them.

Children were an important working part of the family and the community a few years ago. But in today's urban environment, some children are more of a hindrance than a help—and they *feel* this, says Dr. Bruno Bettelheim in the current LOOK.

Is this feeling of being in the way the reason so-many children are anxious and angry? Dr. Bettelheim, a leading authority on problems of the young, thinks so. And he suggests that many of today's kids would grow up happier, healthier and more productive if they were reared in a school-home like an Israeli *kibbutz*.

Everybody knows *what's* happening to today's children. The current LOOK tells *why* it's happening — in "A New Way to Raise Kids." It is the sort of article people have come to expect from LOOK. For LOOK is the only major medium in America today that consistently takes the more thoughtful, reasons-why approach to key issues and trends.

Your advertising tells people *why* they should buy your product or service. Aren't LOOK's 39 million why-interested adult readers the ones most likely to stop, look, read and buy?

LOOK. You'll see why.

309

Advertisements
Inserate
Annonces

311) 312) 'Let us hatch out your card index.'—'I have it all in my head.' Full-page newspaper advertisements for an office organization company. (SWI)

313) Newspaper advertisement for an advertising agency that offers a means of combating the 'price attrition dragon'. (SWI)

314) Full-page newspaper advertisement announcing a meeting organized by an oppositional movement, Coalition for National Priorities. (USA)

315) 316) Full-page newspaper advertisements from a series about the women's magazine MADEMOISELLE. (USA)

317) Black-and-white advertisement soliciting support for SANE, an oppositional political movement. (USA)

318) Full-page newspaper ad for First Federal Savings and Loan Association, warning readers against misleading bank offers. (USA)

311) 312) Ganzseitige Inserate für die Definitiv-Organisation AG. (SWI)

313) Zeitungsinserat für die Werbeagentur KGT, Klöti, Glättli + Tschudi, Zürich, mit einer Offerte, die Preisdrücker-Mentalität zu bekämpfen. Schwarzweiss. (SWI)

314) Ganzseitiges Zeitungsinserat als Einladung einer oppositionellen Bewegung zu einem Treffen unter dem Motto: «Schafft uns das Pentagon vom Hals». (USA)

315) 316) Ganzseitige Zeitungsinserate aus einer Serie für die Frauenzeitschrift MADEMOISELLE. (USA)

317) Schwarzweisses Inserat für eine politische Bewegung. (USA)

318) Ganzseitiges Zeitungsinserat für ein Bankunternehmen mit einer Warnung vor irreführenden Bank-Offerten: «Lesen Sie das nächste Mal die kleingedruckten Zeilen.» (USA)

Artist / Künstler / Artiste:

311) 312) EGON MEICHTRY
313) CLAUS KNÉZY
314) EDWARD SOREL
315) 316) STEVE WALLING
317) EDWARD SOREL/LEN SIROWITZ
318) DICK HENDERSON

Art Director / Directeur artistique:

311) 312) FRED MURER
313) OTTO SCHUMACHER
314) 317) LEN SIROWITZ
315) 316) STEVE WALLING
318) DICK HENDERSON

Agency / Agentur / Agence – Studio:

311) 312) AWG, AG FÜR WERBEPLANUNG UND GESTALTUNG, ZÜRICH
313) KGT-KLÖTI, GLÄTTLI & TSCHUDI AG, ZÜRICH
314) 317) DOYLE DANE BERNBACH, INC., N. Y.
318) COLE, HENDERSON, DRAKE, INC., ATLANTA, GA.

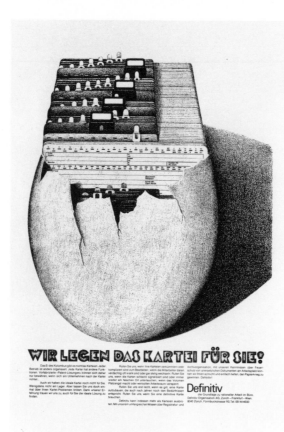

311

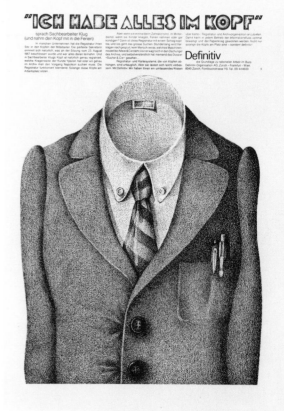

312

315

316

313

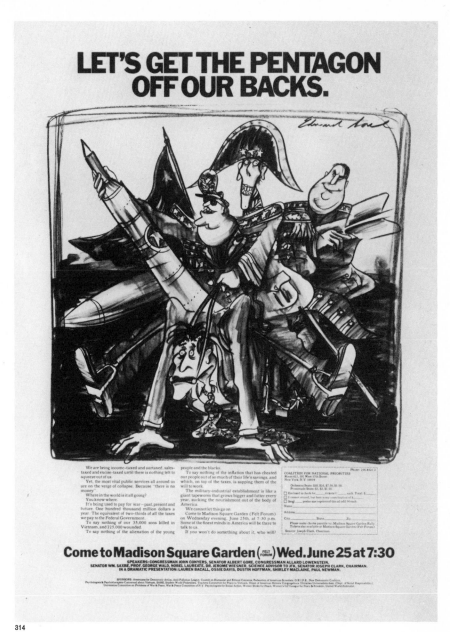

314

317

318

319

THE NEW YORKER

a magazine for people who read

320

Advertisements / Inserate / Annonces

319) 320) Illustration and complete magazine advertisement for THE NEW YORKER. (USA)
321) Full-page newspaper advertisement, with a quiz, for a new encyclopaedic magazine, AGE OF DISCOVERY. (USA)
322) Black-and-white advertisement for Eastern Airlines offering non-stop flights to the sun in Mexico. (USA)

319) 320) Illustration und vollständiges Zeitungsinserat für THE NEW YORKER: « Eine Zeitschrift für Leute, die zu lesen verstehen ». (USA)
321) Ganzseitiges Zeitungsinserat mit einem Quiz für eine neue enzyklopädische Zeitschrift, « Zeitalter der Entdeckungen ». (USA)
322) Schwarzweisses Inserat der Eastern Airlines, die Non-Stop-Flüge zur mexikanischen Sonne anbieten. (USA)

319) 320) Illustration et annonce de revue correspondante, pour l'hebdomadaire THE NEW YORKER, «un magazine pour les gens qui savent lire». (USA)
321) Annonce de presse sur page entière pour une nouvelle revue encyclopédique, intitulée «L'ère des découvertes». (USA)
322) Annonce de la compagnie aérienne Eastern Airlines, offrant des vols directs au soleil du Mexique. Noir et blanc. (USA)

Artist / Künstler / Artiste:

319) 320) SAUL STEINBERG
321) TOMI UNGERER/CLARK FRANKEL
322) PAUL DAVIS/HERBERT KEPKE

Art Director / Directeur artistique:

319) 320) ALEXANDER MOHTARES
321) CLARK FRANKEL
322) HERBERT KEPKE

Agency / Agentur / Agence – Studio:

319) 320) CHIRURG & CAIRNS, INC., NEW YORK
321) 322) YOUNG & RUBICAM, INC., NEW YORK

321

322

3

Booklets

Folders

Catalogues

Invitations

Programmes

Annual Reports

Broschüren

Faltprospekte

Kataloge

Einladungen

Programme

Jahresberichte

Brochures

Dépliants

Catalogues

Invitations

Programmes

Rapports Annuels

323

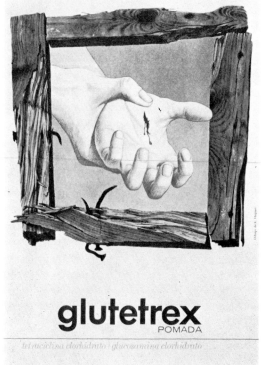

325

327

324

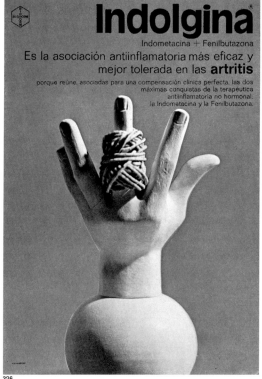

326

328

Booklets / Prospekte
Prospectus

Artist | Künstler | Artiste:

323) MAY NÉAMA
324) GEORGES LEMOINE
325) ENRIC HUGUET
326) JOSÉ PLA NARBONA
327) 328) FRANS KEYSER
329) 330) HARRY SEHRING
331) ROLF HARDER

Art Director | Directeur artistique:

324) GEORGES LEMOINE
325) ENRIC HUGUET
326) JOSÉ PLA NARBONA
327) 328) HENRY VAN HOOF
329) 330) HARRY SEHRING/ALICE KATZ
331) ROLF HARDER/PETER DECKER

Agency | Agentur | Agence – Studio:

324) DELPIRE-ADVICO S.A., PARIS
325) ENRIC HUGUET, BARCELONA
326) STUDIO PLA NARBONA, BARCELONA
329) 330) WILLIAM DOUGLAS MCADAMS, INC., NEW YORK
331) DESIGN COLLABORATIVE LTD., MONTREAL

329

323) Folder for a *Roche* cough syrup. Sepia and black on red. (BEL)
324) Cover of a bulletin issued by a paint manufacturer. Pastel shades. (FRA)
325) Card about an ointment for dermatological uses. Frame in brown shades, red blood. (SPA)
326) Card about a drug used in the treatment of arthritis. Modelled hand, brown ground. (SPA)
327) 328) Cards from a series about the six days of the creation (fig. 327 fourth day, fig. 328 fifth day) for an oral antibiotic. Bright colours. (BEL)
329) 330) Page of a booklet, and inside of a larger folder entitled 'Conflict' in which the booklet was inserted, providing information on the results obtained in animal experiments with a *Roche* tranquillizing drug. (USA)
331) Envelope for a *Roche* calendar mailed at regular intervals to doctors. (CAN)

323) Faltprospekt für einen Hustensirup von *Roche*. Sepia und Schwarz auf rotem Grund. (BEL)
324) Umschlag eines Prospektes für einen Farbenfabrikanten. Pastellfarben. (FRA)
325) Farbige Prospektkarte für eine dermatologische Salbe. Rahmen braun, Blut rot. (SPA)
326) Prospektkarte für ein Medikament gegen Arthritis. Modellierte Hand für Braun. (SPA)
327) 328) Prospektkarten aus einer Serie über die sechs Tage der Schöpfung (Abb. 327 vierter Tag, Abb. 328 fünfter Tag) für ein Antibiotikum. Lebhafte Farben. (BEL)
329) 330) Prospektseite und Innenseite eines grossen Faltprospektes mit dem Titel «Konflikt», in den der kleinere Prospekt eingeheftet war, mit Informationen über die in Tierversuchen mit einem Beruhigungsmittel von *Roche* erzielten Resultate. (USA)
331) Umschlag eines als Prospekt periodisch an Ärzte versandten Kalenders von *Roche*. (CAN)

323) Dépliant pour un sirop *Roche* contre la toux. Sépia et noir sur rouge. (BEL)
324) Couverture d'un bulletin de la Gauthier S.A., Gardinoux, fabricants de peintures. (FRA)
325) Carte polychrome pour un onguent dermatologique des Laboratoires Jorba, Madrid. (SPA)
326) Carte publicitaire pour une préparation de la J. Urisch & Cie. S.A., Barcelone, utilisée dans le traitement de l'arthrite. Main modelée sur fond brun. (SPA)
327) 328) Cartes publicitaires pour un antibiotique de l'Union Chimique Belge S.A., Bruxelles, tirées d'une série consacrée aux six jours de la création. Couleurs vives. (BEL)
329) 330) Page d'un prospectus et vue du grand dépliant le contenant, décrivant les effets d'un tranquillisant *Roche* sur les animaux. (USA)
331) Enveloppe d'un calendrier *Roche* adressé régulièrement aux médecins. (CAN)

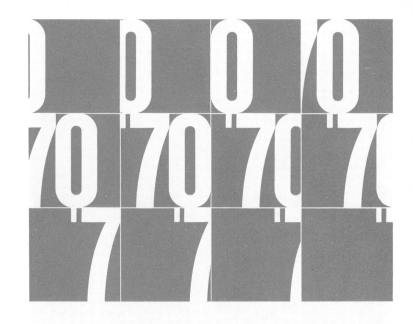

Calendarium Roche 1970

331

330

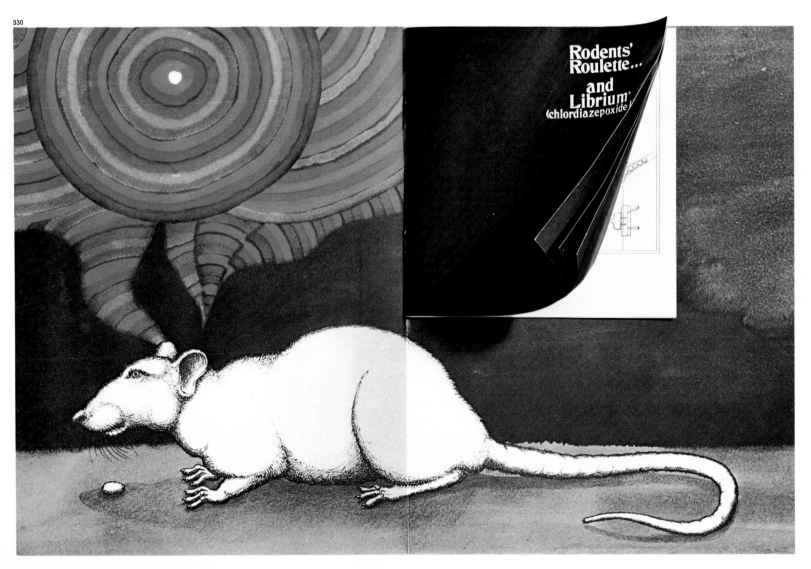

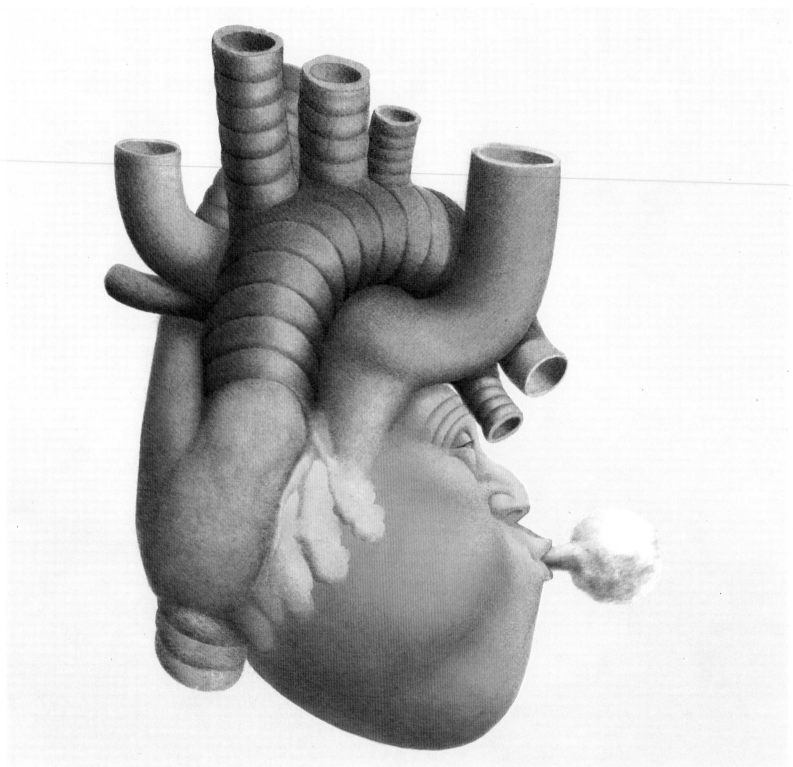

332

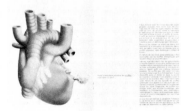

333

334

Artist | Künstler | Artiste:

332)–334) 338) 339) MICHEL GUIRÉ-VAKA/
AGNÈS GEI

335) ARIELLE MATHER/SIDNEY HERMAN

336) 337) LARRY SONS / JIM JACOBS

Art Director | Directeur artistique:

332)–334) 338) 339) AGNÈS GEI

335) SIDNEY HERMAN

336) 337) STAN RICHARDS

Agency | Agentur | Agence – Studio:

332)–334) 338) 339) EDITIONS BOZ, PARIS

335) HERMAN/LEES ASSOC., CAMBRIDGE, MASS.

336) 337) STAN RICHARDS & ASSOC., DALLAS

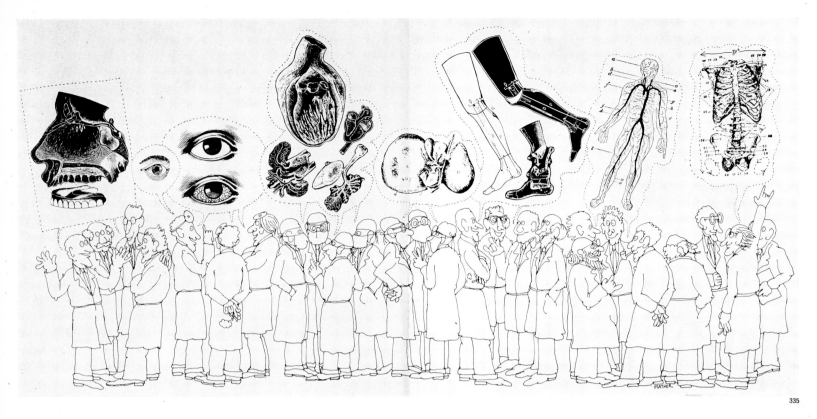

335

332)–334) 338) 339) Illustration and double spreads from a *Hoechst* brochure for distribution to doctors about the diagnostics of the normal heart. (FRA)
335) Inside cover of a programme for a reunion of alumni of the Tufts University School of Medicine. Black and white. (USA)
336) 337) Double spreads (left-hand pages in full colour) from a booklet for Goals, Inc., entitled 'Preventistry', giving a programme of daily oral hygiene. (USA)

332)–334) 338) 339) Illustration und Doppelseiten aus einer *Hoechst*-Broschüre für Ärzte über die Diagnostik eines normal funktionierenden Herzens. (FRA)
335) Innenseite eines Umschlages für das Programm einer Zusammenkunft ehemaliger Schüler einer Universität der medizinischen Fakultät. Schwarzweiss. (USA)
336) 337) Doppelseiten (linke Seiten farbig) aus einer Broschüre für eine Firma der chemischen Industrie mit einem Programm für die tägliche Mundpflege. (USA)

332)–334) 338) 339) Illustration et doubles pages d'une brochure adressée aux médecins par les Laboratoires Hoechst, Paris, et consacrée à la manière de diagnostiquer un cœur fonctionnant normalement. (FRA)
335) Programme (face interne de la couverture) d'une réunion des anciens élèves d'une école de médecine. Noir et blanc. (USA)
336) 337) Doubles pages d'un programme d'hygiène dentaire préventive. (USA)

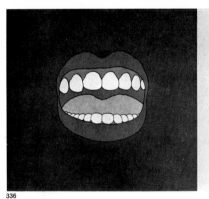

These organisms live on practically every surface of your teeth, between your teeth and gums, and on your tongue, cheeks and the roof of your mouth.

336

The world's champion tooth-brusher, try as he might, can only reach a tiny fraction of the bacterial plaque in his mouth. However, there are easily learned, practical techniques which can get at the rest.
That is the purpose of Preventistry.
After five brief sessions in our office, it takes only a few minutes a night in your home. Follow Preventistry faithfully as instructed and you will be virtually free of new tooth decay and gum disease for as long as you live.

337

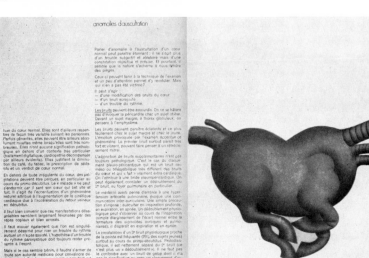

338

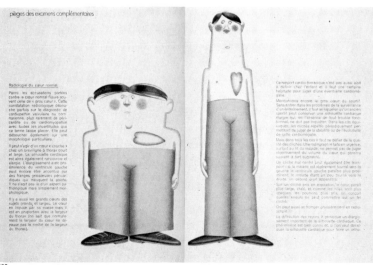

339

340) Type composition of the head of Queen Victoria used on the programme of an exhibition of the Royal College of Art in New York. (GB)
341)–343) Cards from a series for a remedy for coughs and colds. Illustrations in full colour. (FRA)
344) 348) Illustration in black and silver and complete cover of a folder about a *Roche* pharmaceutical for the psychovegetative system. (SWI)
345)–347) Covers of folders, all in full colour, from a series about an ICI pharmaceutical against heart disease and circulatory disorders. (GER)
349) Cover of a folder for a *Roche* vitamin preparation. Black and white. (BEL)

340) Komposition aus Satzschrift des Profils der Königin Viktoria, verwendet im Programm einer Ausstellung des Royal College of Art in New York. (GB)
341)–343) Prospektkarten aus einer Serie für *Salvodex*, ein Mittel für Erwachsene gegen Husten und Erkältungen. Mehrfarbige Illustrationen. (FRA)
344) 348) Illustration in Schwarz und Silber, und ganzer Umschlag eines Fáltprospektes über ein *Roche*-Medikament für das psychovegetative System. (SWI)
345)–347) Faltprospektumschläge, alle mehrfarbig, aus einer Serie für ein Pharmazeutikum der ICI gegen Herzbeschwerden und schlechte Blutzirkulation. (GER)
349) Umschlag eines Faltprospektes für ein *Roche*-Vitaminpräparat. (BEL)

340) Composition typographique de la tête de la reine Victoria, sur le programme d'une exposition du Royal College of Art à New York. (GB)
341)–343) Cartes publicitaires des Laboratoires Salvoxyl S.r.l., d'une série pour un médicament antitussif. Illustrations en couleur. (FRA)
344) 348) Illustration (noir et argent) et couverture d'un dépliant consacré à un médicament *Roche* pour le système neurovégétatif. (SWI)
345)–347) Couvertures de dépliants polychromes, d'une série pour une préparation utilisée dans le traitement des troubles cardiaques et circulatoires. (GER)
349) Couverture d'un dépliant pour une vitamine *Roche*. Noir et blanc. (BEL)

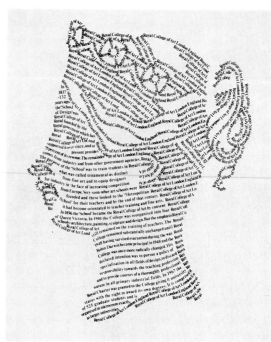

340

344

341

342

343

SALVODEX l'antitussif de l'adulte

SALVODEX l'antitussif de l'adulte

SALVODEX l'antitussif de l'adulte

345

346

347

Artist | Künstler | Artiste:

340) JIM GIBSON
341)–343) MICHEL GUIRÉ-VAKA
344) 348) SILVIA GOESCHKE
345)–347) ATELIER WINTER & BISCHOFF
349) MAY NÉAMA

Art Director | Directeur artistique:

340) JIM GIBSON
341)–343) JEAN-PIERRE GOUREAU
344) 348) JACQUES HAUSER
345)–347) ATELIER WINTER & BISCHOFF

Agency | Agentur | Agence – Studio:

341)–343) EDITIONS BOZ, PARIS

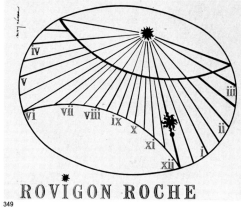

ROVIGON ROCHE

349

348

Booklets / Prospekte / Prospectus

350

351

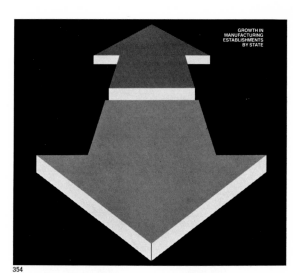

354

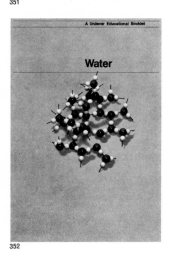

352

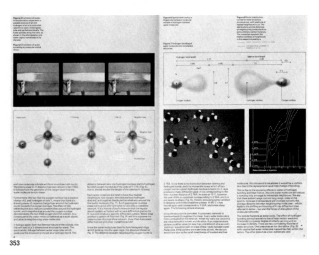

353

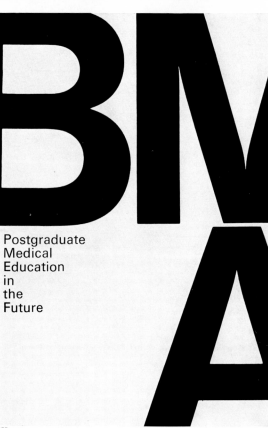

Postgraduate
Medical
Education
in
the
Future

355

350) Card about a drug to help patients put on weight. (BEL)
351) Cover of a booklet about *Agricare* veterinary products. Photographic insets in colour on blue-grey. (GB)
352) 353) Cover and double spread with full-colour illustrations from a *Unilever* educational booklet about water. (GB)
354) Cover of a FORTUNE booklet about the growth of manufacturing establishments. Blue and red arrows. (USA)
355) 357) Cover (and cover with flap) of a report published by *Geigy* on a symposium about medical education. (GB)
356) 358) Cover of a booklet and complete folder from a *Roche* series quoting thinkers—here Kierkegaard—on anxiety. (USA)

350) Prospektkarte über ein Medikament für Gewichtszunahme. (BEL)
351) Umschlag eines Prospektes für *Agricare*-Veterinärprodukte. Farbphotos auf grauem Grund. (GB)
352) 353) Umschlag und Doppelseite mit mehrfarbigen Illustrationen einer Aufklärungsbroschüre über Wasser. (GB)
354) Umschlag einer Broschüre für FORTUNE über die Entwicklung von Fabrikationsbetrieben. Pfeile blau und rot auf Schwarz. (USA)
355) 357) Umschlag mit und ohne Klappe eines *Geigy*-Rapportes über ein Symposium zum Thema der medizinischen Weiterbildung. (GB)
356) 358) Broschürenumschlag und ganzer Prospekt einer *Roche*-Serie über die Angst, grosse Denker zitierend, hier Kierkegaard. (USA)

Art Director | Directeur artistique:

350) HENRY VAN HOOF
351) A.J. BENSTED
352) 353) PETER GAULD
354) GILBERT LESSER
355) 357) BRIAN STONES
356) 358) HARRY SEHRING/ALICE KATZ

Artist | Künstler | Artiste:

350) JOSSE GOFFIN
351) B. BULLEN
352) 353) PETER GAULD
354) GILBERT LESSER
355) 357) ERROL MITCHELL
356) 358) JAMES MCMULLAN/
HARRY SEHRING

Agency | Agentur | Agence – Studio:

351) PFIZER CREATIVE DEPARTMENT, SANDWICH, KENT/GB
355) 357) GEIGY (U.K.) LTD., MANCHESTER/GB
356) 358) WILLIAM DOUGLAS MCADAMS, INC., NEW YORK

356

350) Carte publicitaire de la Sarva S.A., Bruxelles, pour un médicament destiné à aider les patients à prendre du poids. (BEL)

351) Couverture d'un prospectus pour des produits vétérinaires. Photographies en couleur sur fond gris. (GB)

352) 353) Couverture et double page illustrée en couleur, pour une brochure éducative *Unilever* consacrée à l'eau. (GB)

354) Couverture d'un prospectus sur l'expansion des entreprises industrielles. Flèches en bleu et rouge. (USA)

355) 357) Couverture (vue avec les volets) d'un rapport *Geigy* sur un symposium consacré à l'éducation médicale. (GB)

356) 358) Couverture d'un prospectus et vue d'un dépliant, tirés d'une série *Roche* sur le sujet de l'anxiété. (USA)

358

359

361

360

359)–363) Cover, double spreads and pages from two booklets from a series dealing with the medical histories of famous people, here Henry VIII of England and Sir Walter Scott, for Eaton Laboratories. (USA)

364)–366) Double spreads with colour illustrations from a booklet published by a watch manufacturing group. The spreads show the relationship of time divisions to vital functions. (SWI)

367) 368) Covers of brochures from a series about 'patterns of tension', for a Roche drug. (CAN)

369) Cover of a folder about a Syntex cream against dermatitis. Full colour. (CAN)

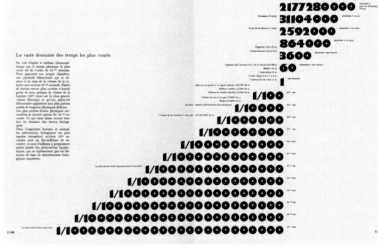

364

367

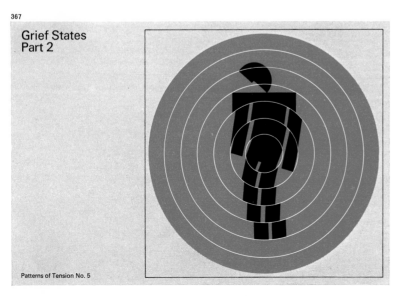

Grief States
Part 2

Patterns of Tension No. 5

The roots
of marital tension

Patterns of Tension No. 6

368

362

363

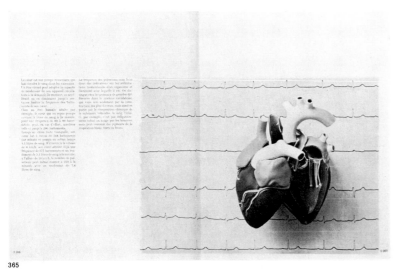

365

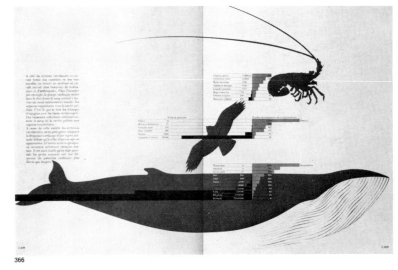

366

369

359)–363) Umschlag, Doppelseiten und Seiten mit Illustrationen aus zwei Prospekten eines chemischen Unternehmens, als Beispiele einer ganzen Serie, die den Krankheitsgeschichten berühmter Persönlichkeiten gewidmet sind, hier Heinrich VIII und Sir Walter Scott. (USA)

364)–366) Doppelseiten mit farbigen Illustrationen aus einem Prospekt einer Gruppe der Uhrenindustrie. Die Darstellungen zeigen den Zeitablauf von lebenswichtigen Funktionen. (SWI)

367) 368) Umschläge aus einer Prospektserie für ein *Roche*-Beruhigungsmittel. (CAN)

369) Umschlag eines Prospektes für *Syntex*, ein Mittel gegen Hauterkrankungen. (CAN)

359)–363) Couverture, doubles pages et pages de deux prospectus publiés par un laboratoire pharmaceutique. Exemples tirés d'une série retraçant l'histoire médicale de personnages célèbres, ici Henri VIII et Sir Walter Scott. (USA)

364)–366) Doubles pages illustrées en couleur, tirées d'un prospectus des Fabriques d'Assortiments Réunies, Le Locle. (SWI)

367) 368) Couvertures de brochures tirées d'une série pour un tranquillisant *Roche*. (CAN)

369) Couverture d'un dépliant pour un onguent dermatologique. Polychrome. (CAN)

Booklets / Prospekte / Prospectus

Artist | Künstler | Artiste:

370) GIOVANNI FERIOLI
371) 372) FRANZISKA SCHMIDT
373) JERROL RICHARDSON/JAMES BRIGHT/
      KEITH BRIGHT & ASSOC.
374)–376) GRAHAM SUTHERLAND/ENZO MARI
377) IAN BRADBERY
378) LARS ROMO

Art Director | Directeur artistique:

370) FRANCO BASSI
371) 372) FRANZISKA SCHMIDT
373) KEITH BRIGHT
374)–376) GIORGIO SOAVI
377) IAN BRADBERY
378) LARS ROMO

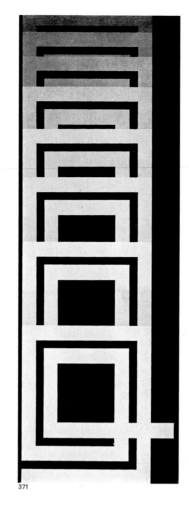

370   371   372

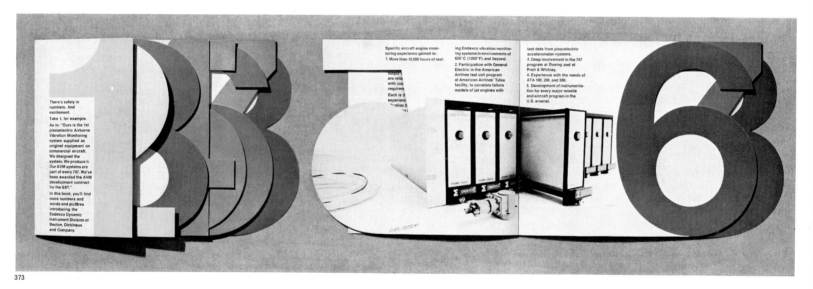

373

Booklets / Prospekte / Prospectus

370) Double spread in black and two greys from a booklet about a range of *Olivetti* electric typewriters. (ITA)

371) 372) Cover (black and white) and double spread (black and white on silver) from an *Olivetti* booklet addressed to prospective shareholders. (GER)

373) Double spread from a brochure with die-cut numbers in various colours describing *Endevco* vibration monitoring equipment for aircraft. (USA)

374)–376) Full-page illustrations by Graham Sutherland and double spread from an *Olivetti* desk calendar. (ITA)

377) Cover of a brochure about *Snowcrete* white Portland cement. Cream shades. (GB)

378) Folder for a building product. Black and mustard. (FIN)

370) Doppelseite eines Prospektes über eine Serie von elektrischen *Olivetti*-Schreibmaschinen. (ITA)

371) 372) Umschlag (schwarzweiss) und Doppelseite (schwarzweiss auf Silber) aus einem für die Aktionäre ausgearbeiteten Prospekt der Deutschen Olivetti GmbH, Frankfurt. (GER)

373) Doppelseite eines Prospektes mit farbigen, gestuft ausgestanzten Nummern, mit Beschreibung der *Endevco*-Kontrollinstrumente für Flugzeuge. (USA)

374)–376) Ganzseitige Illustrationen von Graham Sutherland und Doppelseite aus einem *Olivetti*-Pultkalender. (ITA)

377) Umschlag eines Prospektes für weissen Portlandzement. (GB)

378) Umschlag eines Faltprospektes für ein im Baugewerbe verwendetes Produkt. Schwarz und senffarbig. (FIN)

370) Double page en noir et deux de tons gris, tirée d'un prospectus pour les machines à écrire électriques *Olivetti*. (ITA)

371) 372) Couverture (noir et blanc) et double page (noir et blanc sur argent) d'un prospectus adressé aux actionnaires en puissance par la branche allemande d'*Olivetti*. (GER)

373) Double page d'une brochure décrivant l'équipement *Endevco* destiné à contrôler les vibrations sur les avions. Chiffres de différentes couleurs, découpés au poinçon. (USA)

374)–376) Illustrations de Graham Sutherland sur pages entières et double page d'un agenda de bureau *Olivetti*. (ITA)

377) Couverture d'une brochure pour une marque de ciment. (GB)

378) Couverture d'un dépliant pour un produit utilisé dans l'industrie du bâtiment. Noir et moutarde. (FIN)

374

375

376

377

378

379

380

Booklets / Prospekte / Prospectus

379) 380) Covers of *Knoll International* annual price lists, from a series. (USA)
381) 382) Double spreads from *Knoll International* furniture price lists. Black and white. (USA)
383) Full-page illustration from a booklet for a chemical company with instructions as to how to get to their stand at an industrial fair in London. (GER)
384)–386) Inserts with metallized relief designs contained in a series of mailers, each dealing with a feature of an *Opel* model—here air-cooled disc brakes and a torque converter. (GER)
387)–389) Cover (with moon-surface texture), title page and double spread in colour from a book about CBS reporting of the moon landing in July 1969. (USA)

383

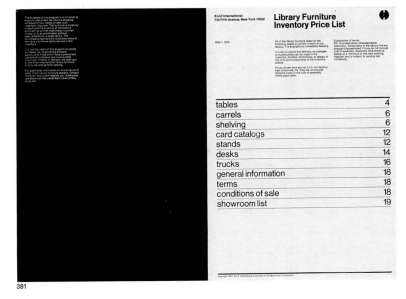

381

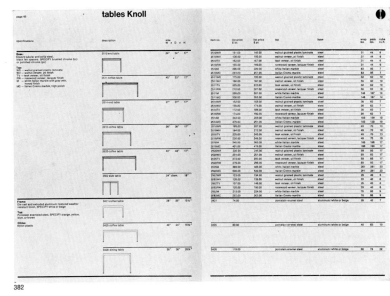

382

379) 380) Umschläge für Preislisten aus einer Serie eines internationalen Unternehmens. (USA)
381) 382) Doppelseiten aus Preislisten für ein internationales Unternehmen, hier für Möbel. (USA)
383) Ganzseitige Illustration aus einem Prospekt der Badischen Anilin- & Soda-Fabrik AG. (GER)
384)–386) Beilagen mit metallisierten Reliefs aus einer Serie von per Post versandten Prospekten; jeder Prospekt beschreibt einen Bestandteil der *Opel*-Modelle, hier belüftete Scheibenbremsen und einen Drehmomentwandler. (GER)
387)–389) Umschlag (mit mondboden-ähnlicher Struktur), Titelseite und farbige Doppelseite aus einem Buch über die CBS-Reportagen anlässlich der Mondlandung im Juli 1969. (USA)

379) 380) Couvertures de tarifs *Knoll International*. Exemples tirés d'une série. (USA)
381) 382) Doubles pages de tarifs de meubles *Knoll International*. Noir et blanc. (USA)
383) Illustration sur page entière, tirée du prospectus d'une fabrique de produits chimiques et indiquant la position de son stand à une foire industrielle de Londres. (GER)
384)–386) Encarts, portant des motifs métallisés en relief, insérés dans une série de prospectus consacrés à l'équipement des voitures *Opel*. (GER)
387)–389) Couverture (texture lunaire), page de titre et double page en couleur d'une plaquette consacrée aux reportages CBS sur l'alunissage de juillet 1969. (USA)

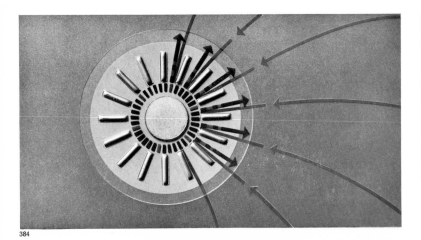

384

387

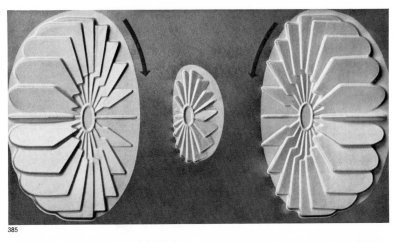

385

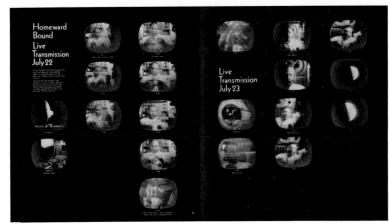

388

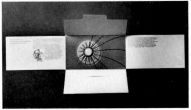

386

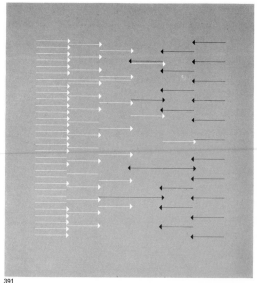

390

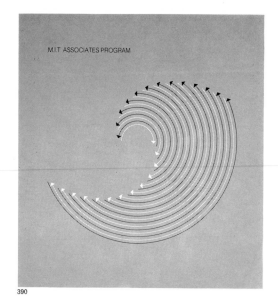

391

Colt Industries Inc First Quarter 1969

392

Colt Industries Inc Midyear Results 1969
and Annual Meeting
Summary

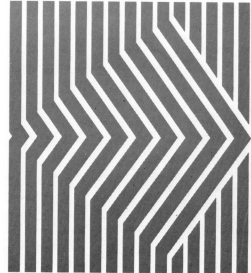

393

PROBLEMATICAL
RECREATIONS[11]

394

20.

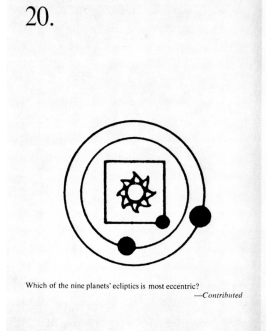

Which of the nine planets' ecliptics is most eccentric?
—*Contributed*

395

21.

The local weather forecaster says "no rain" and his record is 2/3 accuracy of prediction. But the Federal Meteorological Service predicts rain and *their* record is 3/4. *A priori* it's as likely as not to rain. What is the chance of rain?   —*Contributed*

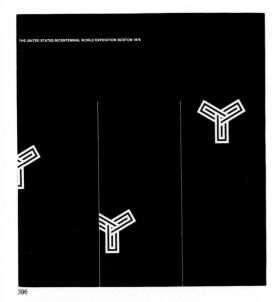

396

397

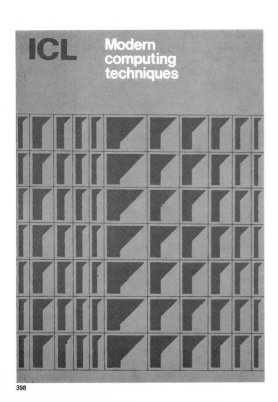

398

399

390) 391) Cover and page from a booklet about the contacts maintained by Massachusetts Institute of Technology with industry. Black and white on grey-brown. (USA)

392) 393) Covers of small quarterly business reports issued by Colt Industries, Inc. Fig. 392 with olive design, Fig. 393 with blue design, black lettering. (USA)

394) 395) Cover and double spread from a booklet of problems, one of a series issued by Litton Industries. (USA)

396) Cover of a brochure about the theme, site and concept of a projected world exhibition. Red and white. (USA)

397) Cover of a packaging catalogue. Purple, blue and green circles, with putty and black on red. (SWI)

398) Folder from a series for International Computers Ltd. Two colours. (GB)

399) Direct-mail poster about a Thanksgiving Day Parade broadcast co-sponsored by U.S. Steel. Red turkey. (USA)

390) 391) Umschlag und Seite eines Prospektes eines technischen Institutes über ihre mit der Industrie gepflegten Kontakte. Schwarzweiss auf Graubraun. (USA)

392) 393) Umschläge zweier Quartalsrapporte der Colt Industries Inc. an ihre Aktionäre. Abb. 392 mit olivfarbiger Zeichnung Abb. 393 mit blauer Zeichnung, beide mit schwarzer Schrift. (USA)

394) 395) Umschlag und Doppelseite aus einer Broschüre mit Rechenrätseln. Beispiel aus einer Serie. (USA)

396) Umschlag einer Broschüre über Thema, Ort und Gestaltung einer geplanten Weltausstellung. Weiss auf Rot. (USA)

397) Umschlag eines Verpackungskataloges von Max Binkert & Co., Laufenburg. Farbige Kreise, roter Grund. (SWI)

398) Prospekt aus einer Serie für International Computers Ltd. Zweifarbig. (GB)

399) Per Post versandtes Plakat über eine Radioreportage am amerikanischen Dankfest. Roter Truthahn. (USA)

390) 391) Couverture et page d'un prospectus consacré aux contacts entre le Massachusetts Institute of Technology et l'industrie. Noir et blanc sur gris-brun. (USA)

392) 393) Couvertures de petits rapports trimestriels des Colt Industries, Inc. Ill. 392 : dessin en vert olive ; ill. 393 : dessin en bleu, titre en noir. (USA)

394) 395) Couverture et double page d'un recueil de devinettes mathématiques. Exemple tiré d'une série. (USA)

396) Couverture d'une brochure consacrée à un projet d'exposition universelle. Noir et blanc. (USA)

397) Couverture d'un catalogue d'emballages. Cercles mauves, bleus et verts sur fond rouge. (SWI)

398) Dépliant tiré d'une série pour une marque d'ordinateurs. Deux couleurs. (GB)

399) Prospectus sous forme d'affiche, pour un reportage radiodiffusé. Dinde rouge. (USA)

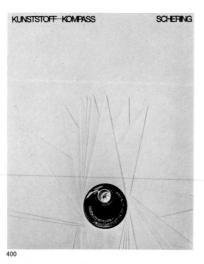

400

401

402

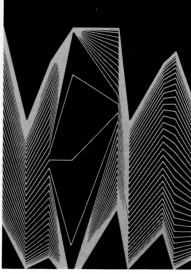

403

404

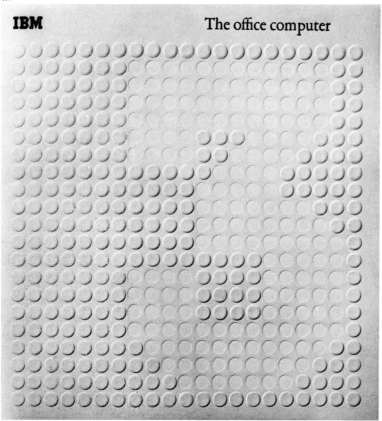

405

l'un de vos camions n'est-il pas un peu petit ?

406

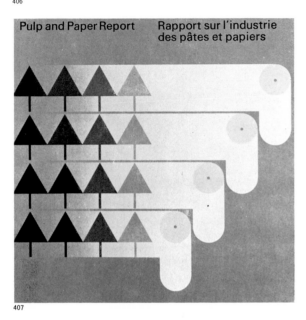

Pulp and Paper Report — Rapport sur l'industrie des pâtes et papiers

407

408

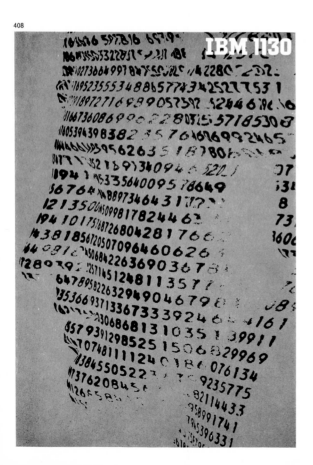

IBM 1130

409

400) 401) Embossed cover and double spread from a brochure about galvanized plastics. The compass in the die-cut hole is attached to the inside back cover. (GER)
402) 403) Cover and double spread from an IBM booklet showing experiments in motion graphics. Yellow and deep pink, black type matter. (USA)
404) 405) Embossed covers in two blacks and two whites for booklets from a series supplying information on IBM office computers. (USA)
406) From a series of large direct-mail-folders about the *Renault* range of trucks. (FRA)
407) Cover of a report issued by the Canadian Pulp and Paper Association. (CAN)
408) Cover of a brochure about an IBM computing system. Black and white on blue. (GB)
409) Die-cut folder about *Volkswagen* cars issued by a garage and containing a lottery ticket and a voucher for a free check. (SWI)

400) 401) Blindgeprägter Umschlag und Doppelseite einer Broschüre der Schering AG, Berlin, über galvanisiertes Plastikmaterial. Der Kompass, der durch die ausgestanzten Löcher in den Seiten erscheint, ist auf der dritten Umschlagseite befestigt. (GER)
402) 403) Umschlag und Doppelseite aus einem IBM-Prospekt. Gelb und Dunkelrosa. (USA)
404) 405) Blindgeprägte Umschläge zweier Prospekte mit Informationen über IBM-Datenverarbeitungsmaschinen. Ein Umschlag in zwei Schwarztönen, der andere in zwei Weisstönen. (USA)
406) Aus einer Serie grosser, per Post versandter Prospekte über *Renault*-Lastwagen. (FRA)
407) Umschlag eines Rapportes über den gesteigerten Verbrauch an Papierstoff und Papieren. (CAN)
408) Umschlag eines Prospektes über IBM-Datenverarbeitung. Schwarzweiss auf Blau. (GB)
409) Ausgestanzter Faltprospekt über *Volkswagen* der Amag AG, Schinznach, mit Gratislos und Talon für eine kostenlose Zustandsprüfung für Besitzer von Volkswagen. (SWI)

400) 401) Couverture gaufrée et double page d'une brochure consacrée aux plastiques galvanisés. La boussole, visible sur chaque page à travers les trous poinçonnés, est fixée sur la face interne du verso de la couverture. (GER)
402) 403) Couverture et double page d'un prospectus IBM. Jaune et rose, texte en noir. (USA)
404) 405) Couvertures gaufrées, l'une dans deux nuances de noir, l'autre dans deux nuances de blanc, de prospectus documentaires sur les ordinateurs de bureau IBM. (USA)
406) D'une série de grands dépliants pour les camions *Renault*. (FRA)
407) Couverture d'un rapport sur les usages de la pâte à papier et du papier. (CAN)
408) Couverture d'une brochure sur les ordinateurs IBM. Noir et blanc sur bleu. (GB)
409) Dépliant découpé au poinçon d'un distributeur de voitures *Volkswagen* contenant un billet de loterie et un bon pour un contrôle gratuit. (SWI)

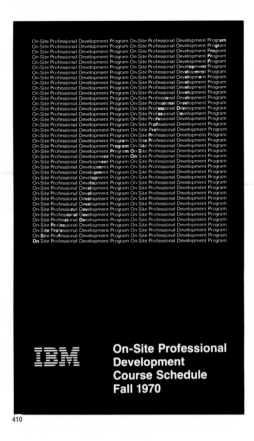

410

411

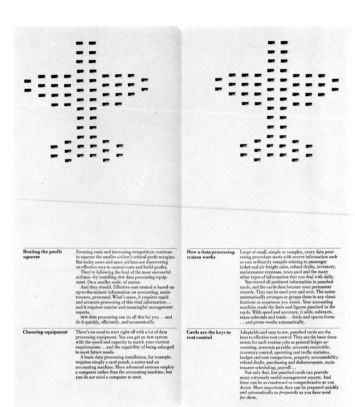

412

Booklets / Prospekte
Prospectus

413

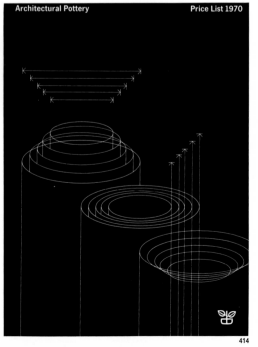

414

415

416

417

418

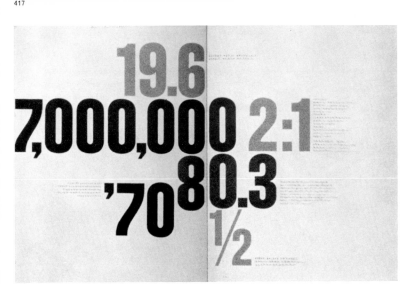

420

Buying is only half the battle.
Making the right investment at the right time isn't quite enough to insure success, however. You have to sell at the right time, too.
The principle that guides us here is that when you ride a tiger, the best time to dismount is not when it has finished its meal, but while it is still feeding.

419

Fare Quote/Ticketing...a
new computer program that
puts the passenger first

421   422

410) Cover of a course schedule for IBM. Black and white. (USA)
411) 412) Cover and double spread from an IBM booklet. (USA)
413) Cover of a booklet on an institute for human relations. (USA)
414) Cover of a price list for architectural pottery. (USA)
415) Cover of a bi-monthly publication of Central Mortgage and Housing Corp. Red on yellow, white title. (CAN)
416) Cover of a booklet about national parks issued by a governmental department. Olive and orange design. (CAN)
417)–419) Black-and-white illustrations and double spread from booklets about an investment service of the Vestaur Corp. (USA)
420) Double spread from a brochure for Chunichi Newspapers. (JAP)
421) 422) Cover and first page of an IBM booklet on ticketing. (USA)

410) Umschlag eines Programmes für einen IBM-Kurs. (USA)
411) 412) Umschlag und Doppelseite eines IBM-Prospektes. (USA)
413) Umschlag eines Prospektes für ein Institut für zwischenmenschliche Beziehungen. (USA)
414) Umschlag eines Katalogs über Fassaden-Verkleidungen. (USA)
415) Farbiger Umschlag der Broschüre einer Bausparkasse. (CAN)
416) Umschlag einer Broschüre über Nationalpärke. Farbig. (CAN)
417–419) Schwarzweisse Illustrationen und Doppelseite aus Prospekten über Kapitalanlage-Beratung. (USA)
420) Doppelseite eines Prospektes für eine Zeitung. (JAP)
421) 422) Umschlag und Innenseite einer IBM-Broschüre über automatisierte Billetausgabe. Schwarz auf Braun. (USA)

410) Couverture du programme d'un cours IBM. Noir et blanc. (USA)
411) 412) Couverture et double page d'un prospectus IBM. (USA)
413) Couverture d'un prospectus consacré aux activités d'un institut en faveur des relations humaines. (USA)
414) Couverture du tarif d'une entreprise de recouvrement de façades. (USA)
415) Couverture d'une publication bimensuelle. Polychrome. (CAN)
416) Couverture d'une brochure sur les parcs nationaux. (CAN)
417)–419) Illustrations en noir et double page de prospectus en faveur des services d'une société d'investissements. (USA)
420) Double page d'une brochure pour un journal. (JAP)
421) 422) Couverture et première page d'un prospectus IBM. (USA)

423

424

425

426

427

428

429

423)–429) Envelope and examples of the cards contained in it, each of which supplies information on one of the services of a Parisian bank. All designs in colour. (FRA)

430) 431) Double spread and illustration from a booklet about a computer time sharing system, for International Data Highways Ltd. (GB)

432) 433) Double spread and page from a booklet about the genesis of the new symbol of the *Rhône-Poulenc* group. Colour illustrations. (FRA)

423)–429) Kuvert und Beispiele von darin enthaltenen Karten, wovon jede über eine spezielle Abteilung einer Bank informiert. Alle Illustrationen mehrfarbig. (FRA)

430) 431) Doppelseite und Illustration aus einer Broschüre über Datenverarbeitung. (GB)

432) 433) Doppelseite und Seite aus einem Prospekt über die Entstehungsgeschichte des neuen Firmenzeichens eines durch Fusion gebildeten Unternehmens. Farbige Zeichnungen. (FRA)

423)–429) Enveloppe et exemples des cartes qui y sont contenues, décrivant les différents services de la Banque Nationale de Paris. Illustrations polychromes. (FRA)

430) 431) Double page et illustration d'une brochure sur le traitement de l'information. (GB)

432) 433) Double page et page d'une brochure sur la génèse d'un nouvel emblème pour le groupe *Rhône-Poulenc*. Illustrations polychromes. (FRA)

432

...un jour, Rhône et Poulenc s'unirent pour former Rhône-Poulenc.

42 ans après, le groupe s'étant étendu, les filiales étaient réparties dans le monde entier.

C'est alors qu'on eut une idée. Et elle était bonne. Il fallait créer un signe de reconnaissance, un symbole de cohésion et de dynamisme.

sur les camions...

sur les enveloppes...

dans les journaux...

449

In der vorliegenden Druck-schrift wird dem Leser der Typ des Original-Gradar® Rasters in Wort und Bild vorge-stellt. Wie beiläufig ergab sich da-bei der Blick nach links und nach rechts. Denn einmal sind die Funkti-onen eines Rasterpunktes nicht für alle Zeiten festgelegt und zum ande-ren ist der Vorgang des Rastersehens interessant genug, um hier einmal eingehend beschrieben zu werden. So hoffen wir, mit dieser „Text-Trilogie" und den ergänzen-den Bild-Beispielen unse-ren Geschäftsfreunden einigen Nutzen zu bieten.

450

451

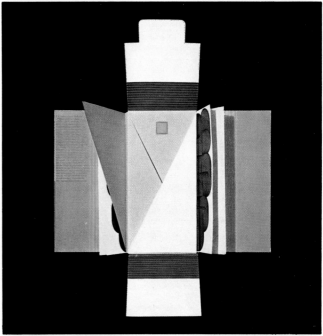

452

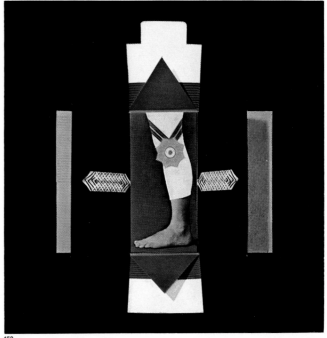

453

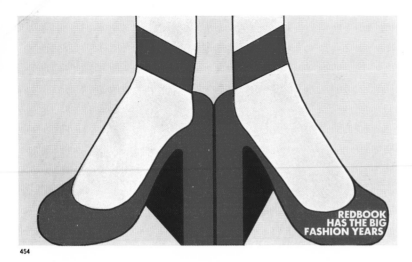

454

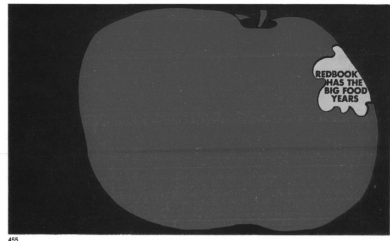

455

454) 455) Two direct-mail space promotion folders for REDBOOK magazine, here referring to fashions and foods. (USA)

456) 457) Posters on various grades of paper forming a special edition of a publication issued at intervals by Champion Papers. (USA)

458) Cover of a brochure about newspaper advertising in THE NEW YORK TIMES. (USA)

459) One side of a concertina-type folder for IBM. The design was produced by a light trace during the composition of the copy for the folder on an IBM composing machine. (SWI)

460) Mailer about a new plant erected by the papermakers Blake, Moffitt & Towne. Blue, black and purple. (USA)

461) Cover of a REDBOOK guide to food refrigeration, with recipes. Full colour. (USA)

462) Cover of a booklet about department store advertising in REDBOOK magazine. Small insets in full colour. (USA)

454) 455) Zwei Prospekte zur Inseratenwerbung für die Zeitschrift REDBOOK, hier für Mode und Lebensmittel. (USA)

456) 457) In Prospektmappe versandte Plakate auf verschiedenen Papierqualitäten für einen Papierfabrikanten. (USA)

458) Umschlag eines Prospektes über publizierte Inserate, als Inseratenwerbung für THE NEW YORK TIMES. (USA)

459) Eine Seite eines Leporello-Faltprospektes für IBM. Die Leuchtspur gibt die Bewegungen des Druckkopfes einer IBM-Setzmaschine wieder. (SWI)

460) Geschlossener und geöffneter Prospekt über den Neubau eines Papierfabrikanten. Schwarzer und violetter Pfeil auf blauem Grund. (USA)

461) Umschlag eines Prospektes für eine Zeitschrift mit Vorschlägen für erfrischende Menus zur Sommerzeit. (USA)

462) Umschlag eines Prospektes zur Inserentenwerbung, an Warenhäuser gerichtet, für die Zeitschrift REDBOOK. (USA)

454) 455) Deux dépliants pour la publicité (mode et alimentation) dans la revue REDBOOK. (USA)

456) 457) Affiches imprimées sur différents types de papier et rassemblées en un portefeuille publicitaire pour un fabricant de papier. (USA)

458) Couverture d'un prospectus pour la publicité dans THE NEW YORK TIMES. (USA)

459) Une page d'un prospectus en accordéon. La trace lumineuse enregistre le mouvement de la tête imprimante d'une composeuse IBM. (SWI)

460) Prospectus présentant la nouvelle usine d'un fabricant de papier. Bleu, noir et mauve. (USA)

461) Couverture d'un recueil de recettes rafraîchissantes, publié par la revue REDBOOK. Polychrome. (USA)

462) Couverture d'un prospectus pour la publicité en faveur des grands magasins dans la revue REDBOOK. (USA)

456

457

458

Artist | Künstler | Artiste:

454) 455) VALERIE KLECKNER
456) 457) ARNOLD SAKS
458) ARNOLD KUSHNER
459) EDGAR REINHARD
460) JIM RICHARDSON/JOHN MCCARTY
461) ARNOLD VARGA/VALERIE KLECKNER
462) JOEL BENAY/VALERIE KLECKNER

Booklets / Prospekte / Prospectus

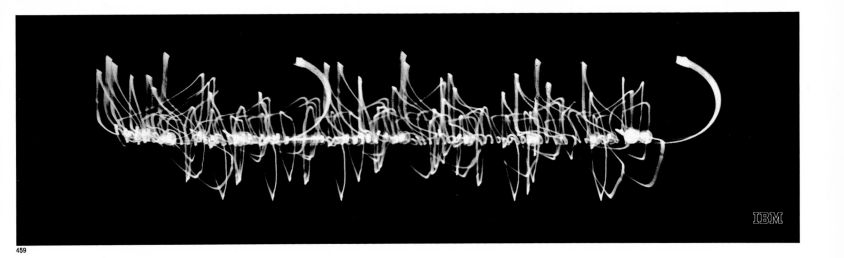

459

460

461

462

Art Director / Directeur artistique:

454) 455) 461) 462) VALERIE KLECKNER
456) 457) ARNOLD SAKS
458) ANDREW KNER
459) EDGAR REINHARD
460) JIM RICHARDSON

Agency / Agentur / Agence – Studio:

460) JAMES RICHARDSON & ASSOC., SEATTLE, WA.
461) 462) REDBOOK PROMOTION DEPT., NEW YORK

463

464

portrait of...who?

Artist | Künstler | Artiste:

463) 464) ROD SPRINGETT/KLAUS WUTTKE
465) 466) TED ZEIGLER/EDDIE BYRD
467)–469) FRED O. BECHLEN
470)–472) PRECOLUMBIAN/KEITH GODARD
473) 474) VALERIE KLECKNER/MONA MARK
475) FRITZ GOTTSCHALK
476) JACKIE LAFLEUR

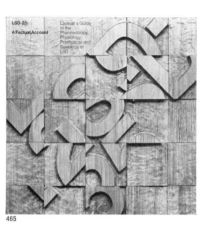

465

466

463) 464) Cover and spread of a booklet on programmes of Television Recordings Ltd. Relief attached to back cover. (GB)

465) 466) Cover and double spread from a government guide to LSD. (USA)

467)–469) Cover and spreads of a booklet for Nippon Educational Television. (JAP)

470)–472) Cover and spreads from a catalogue for a Precolumbian art exhibition in the Museum of Primitive Art. (USA)

473) 474) Cover and folder on cosmetics advertising in REDBOOK magazine. (USA)

475) Catalogue cover for an exhibition in the Montreal Museum of Fine Arts. (CAN)

476) Cover of a booklet about a silent film programme sponsored by The Museum of Modern Art. Black/white/pink. (USA)

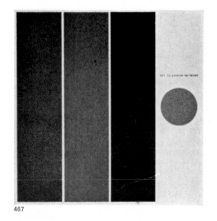

467

468

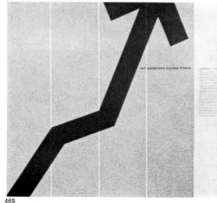

469

Art Director | Directeur artistique:

463) 464) ROD SPRINGETT/KLAUS WUTTKE
465) 466) EDDIE BYRD
467)–469) FRED O. BECHLEN
470)–472) JULIA JONES
473) 474) VALERIE KLECKNER
475) FRITZ GOTTSCHALK
476) JOHN T. ENGEMAN

Agency | Agentur | Agence – Studio:

463) 464) SPRINGETT, WUTTKE LTD., LONDON
467)–469) KOIDE ADVERTISING ART, INC., TOKYO
475) GOTTSCHALK & ASH LTD., MONTREAL
476) TASI, GELBERG, PESANELLI, INC., WASHINGTON, D.C.

463) 464) Umschlag und Doppelseite eines Prospektes für Fernsehprogramme, mit weissem Relief. (GB)

465) 466) Umschlag und Doppelseite einer Aufklärungsbroschüre über LSD. (USA)

467)–469) Umschlag und Doppelseiten eines Prospektes für das Schul-Fernsehen. Beige und Grau, Kreis rot. (JAP)

470)–472) Umschlag und Doppelseiten eines Katalogs für ein Museum. (USA)

473) 474) Umschlag und auseinandergefaltete Innenseite eines Prospektes zur Inserentenwerbung in der Kosmetikbranche für die Zeitschrift REDBOOK. (USA)

475) Umschlag eines Katalogs für eine Ausstellung in einem Kunstmuseum. (CAN)

476) Umschlag der Broschüre eines Museums für ein Stummfilmprogramm. (USA)

463) 464) Couverture et page d'un prospectus pour les programmes d'un émetteur de TV, avec relief blanc. (GB)

465) 466) Couverture et double page d'une brochure officielle sur le LSD. (USA)

467)–469) Couverture et doubles pages d'un prospectus pour la TV éducative. (JAP)

470)–472) Couverture et doubles pages du catalogue d'une exposition d'art précolombien à New York. (USA)

473) 474) Couverture et vue d'un dépliant pour la publicité en faveur des produits de beauté dans une revue. (USA)

475) Couverture d'un catalogue d'exposition. (CAN)

476) Couverture d'un prospectus pour la présentation de films muets dans un musée. Noir, blanc et rose. (USA)

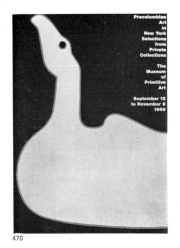

470

471

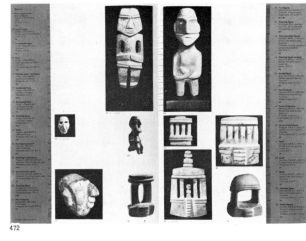

472

473

474

475

476

477) Direct-mail folder for the children's book section of THE NEW YORK TIMES. Illustration black, orange and blue. (USA)
478) Direct-mail folder to advertisers about the spring garden supplement of THE NEW YORK TIMES. (USA)
479) Holiday announcement card for a printer. (BEL)
480) Cover of the programme of a music festival at the Venice Biennale. Red and yellow lettering. (ITA)
481) Press folder for the city of Bonn. Silver with bright colours in the eye of the 'o'. (GER)
482) Cover of a brochure about films broadcast by CBS television. Muted colours. (USA)
483) Catalogue cover for an AIGA graphic design exhibition. (USA)
484) 485) Sheets from a programme for a series of concerts. Red numbers on brown shades. (GER)

477) Prospekt für die Kinderbücher-Beilage einer New Yorker Zeitung. Illustration in Schwarz, Orange und Blau. (USA)
478) Prospekt einer Zeitung zur Inserentenwerbung für ihre Sonderausgabe «Gartengeräte für den Frühling». (USA)
479) Farbige-Ferien-Meldekarte einer Druckerei. (BEL)
480) Umschlag eines Programmes für ein Musikfestival am Biennale von Venedig. Schrift rot und gelb auf Schwarz. (ITA)
481) Mappe des Werbe- und Verkehrsamtes der Stadt Bonn für die Presse. Grund Silber, Bunzen des «o» buntfarbig. (GER)
482) Umschlag eines Prospektes über im Fernsehen gezeigte Filme der CBS. Matte Farbtöne. (USA)
483) Katalogumschlag für eine Graphik-Ausstellung. (USA)
484) 485) Seiten aus einem Programm für verschiedene, vom Bayerischen Rundfunk durchgeführte Konzerte. (GER)

477

478

479

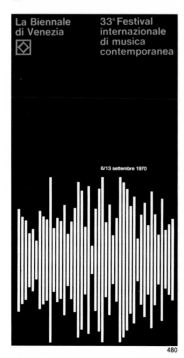

480

481

Artist / Künstler / Artiste:

477) BILL SOKOL
478) SANDY HOFFMANN/PAUL KUTIL
479) MAY NÉAMA
480) SALVATORE GREGORIETTI
481) WALTER SEXAUER/DÖRNEMANN
482) GILBERT STONE/JUDY PERRY
483) PETER BRADFORD
484) 485) WALTER TAFELMAIER

Art Director / Directeur artistique:

477) BILL SOKOL
478) ANDREW KNER
480) SALVATORE GREGORIETTI
481) WALTER SEXAUER
482) JUDY PERRY
483) PETER BRADFORD
484) WALTER TAFELMAIER

Agency / Agentur / Agence – Studio:

480) UNIMARK INTERNATIONAL, MILAN
483) PETER BRADFORD & ASSOC., NEW YORK

477) Dépliant pour la rubrique consacrée aux livres d'enfants dans The New York Times. Illustration en noir, orange et bleu. (USA)
478) Dépliant pour la publicité dans un supplément du New York Times consacré aux jardins. (USA)
479) Carte de l'Imprimerie Georges Thone, Bruxelles, annonçant la date des vacances annuelles. Illustration polychrome. (BEL)
480) Couverture du programme d'un festival de musique à la Biennale de Venise. Texte en rouge et jaune. (ITA)
481) Dépliant touristique pour la ville de Bonn. (GER)
482) Couverture d'une brochure sur les films présentés par une chaine de télévision. Couleurs passées. (USA)
483) Couverture du catalogue d'une exposition d'art graphique. (USA)
484) 485) Pages du programme d'une série de concerts. Chiffres en rouge sur fond brun. (GER)

AIGA Communication Graphics 1968

482

483

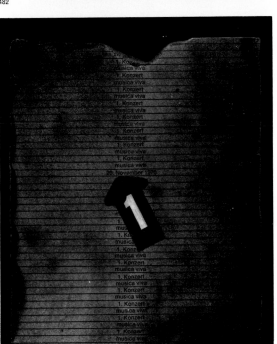

484

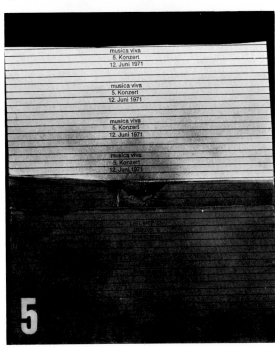

485

486

487

489

490

Booklets / Prospekte / Prospectus

486) 'Diploma' conferred for correct answers to a television quiz. (GER)

487) Cover of a winter programme of events organized by Corning Glass Works. (USA)

488) 492) Double spread and illustration from a programme for the theatres of Essen. (GER)

489) Cover of the winter programme of a radio and television authority. Full colour. (GER)

490) Programme for a showing of films by black artists in the Jewish Museum. (USA)

491) Double spread from a programme of performances in the theatres of Essen. (GER)

488

491

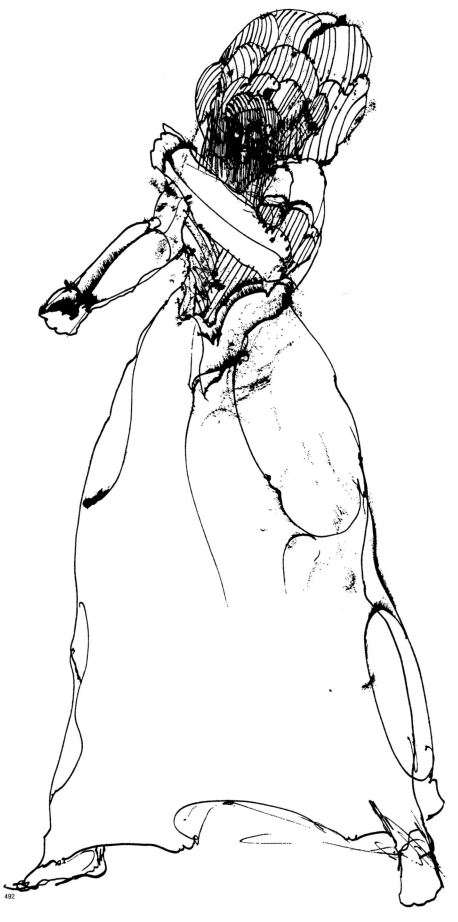

492

486) Für korrekte Lösung eines Fernseh-Quiz vom Norddeutschen Rundfunk überreichtes «Diplom». (GER)

487) Winter-Unterhaltungsplan einer Glasfabrik. (USA)

488) 492) Doppelseite und Zeichnung aus einem Winterprogramm der Bühnen der Stadt Essen. (GER)

489) Mehrfarbiger Umschlag für ein Winterprogramm des Bayerischen Rundfunks. (GER)

490) Spielplan-Programm für von schwarzen Künstlern gedrehte Filme in einem jüdischen Museum. (USA)

491) Schwarzweisse Doppelseite aus einem Spielplan für Aufführungen der Bühnen der Stadt Essen. (GER)

486) «Diplôme» remis aux gagnants d'un concours à la télévision. (GER)

487) Couverture du programme des manifestations organisées par une verrerie. (USA)

488) 492) Double page et illustration, tirées d'un programme de théâtre. (GER)

489) Couverture polychrome d'un programme de radio et de télévision. (GER)

490) Programme pour la présentation dans un musée juif de films réalisés par des artistes noirs. (USA)

491) Double page d'un programme de théâtre. (GER)

493

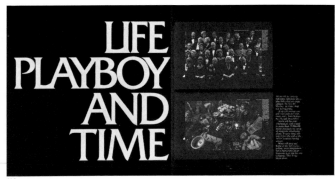

493a

Artist | Künstler | Artiste:

493) 493a) JAMES BENEDICT
494) 495) 497) 498) GÜNTHER KIESER
496) STANISLAW ZAGORSKI
499) 500) MILTON GLASER

Art Director | Directeur artistique:

493) 493a) JAMES BENEDICT
496) JOHN CHANNELL
499) 500) MILTON GLASER

Agency | Agentur | Agence – Studio:

493) 493a) HURVIS, BINZER & CHURCHILL, INC., CHICAGO
499) PUSH PIN STUDIOS, INC., NEW YORK

494

hr
Eine Auswahl
von Sendungen
im Januar
1970

Hessischer Rundfunk Hörfunk

495

496

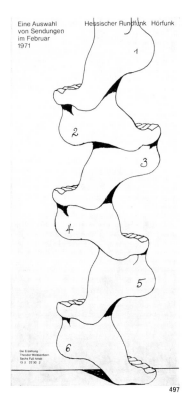

497

Eine Auswahl
von Sendungen
im Februar
1971

Hessischer Rundfunk Hörfunk

498

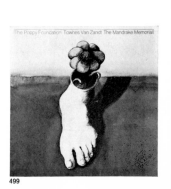

499

493) 493a) Cover and spread from a mailer for *Arvin*, makers of radios and tape recorders. (USA)

494) 495) 497) 498) Covers and double spreads from monthly programmes of the Hessian radio. Black and white. (GER)

496) Colour cover of a catalogue of books on economics. (USA)

499) 500) Complete cover and cover design for a booklet about a popular singer. (USA)

493) 493a) Umschlag und Doppelseite eines Prospektes für einen Hersteller von Radioapparaten und Tonbandgeräten. (USA)

494) 495) 497) 498) Schwarzweisse Umschläge und Doppelseiten aus Monats-Programmen des Hessischen Rundfunks. (GER)

496) Mehrfarbiger Umschlag eines Bücherkataloges. (USA)

499) 500) Vollständiger Umschlag und Illustration einer Broschüre über einen populären Sänger. (USA)

493) 493a) Couverture et double page d'un prospectus pour un fabricant d'appareils de radio et de magnétophones. (USA)

494) 495) 497) 498) Couvertures et doubles pages de programmes mensuels d'un émetteur radiophonique. (GER)

496) Couverture d'un catalogue d'ouvrages d'économie. (USA)

499) 500) Couverture, et son illustration, d'un prospectus consacré à un chanteur à la mode. (USA)

500

501

502

503

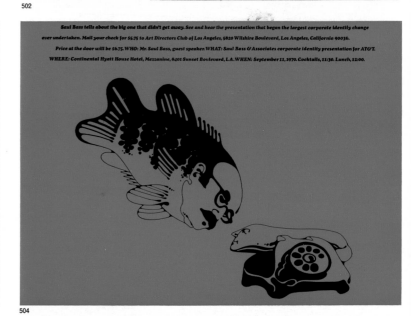

504

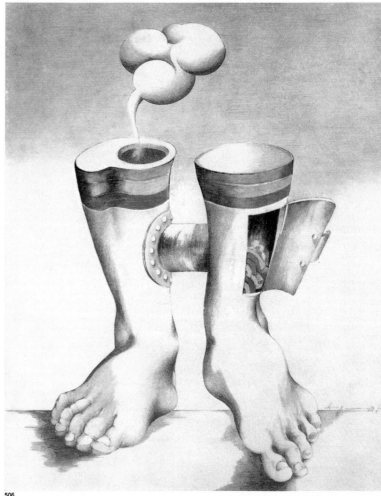

506

Artist | Künstler | Artiste:

501) 502) JERRY HERRING
503) JACK SUMMERFORD, BARBERA ZILLER (designers)
504) DON WELLER
505) WARREN WEBER/DON TROUSDELL
506) 507) EBERHARD EGGERS/HANS-D. NEUMANN
508) TED ZEIGLER/STEVE CHAPMAN

Art Director | Directeur artistique:

501) 502) STAN RICHARDS
503) JACK SUMMERFORD
504) DENNIS JUETT/DON WELLER
505) JIM HESS
506) 507) HANS-D. NEUMANN
508) STEVE CHAPMAN

Agency | Agentur | Agence – Studio:

501) 502) STAN RICHARDS & ASSOCIATES, DALLAS
503) CREATIVE DIRECTIONS, INC., DALLAS
504) WELLER & JUETT, INC., LOS ANGELES
505) GRAPHICS GROUP, INC., ATLANTA, GA.
506) 507) INTRODUCT WERBEAGENTUR, HANNOVER
508) BEVERIDGE & ASSOCIATES, INC., WASHINGTON, D.C.

This man, born of middle class parents, had long hair and a beard.
He was a pacifist, a member of a minority group, a wanderer and considered
a social drop-out. He bathed infrequently, worked with His hands and was hated by the
establishment, who eventually executed Him. To learn more about Him attend Senior Sunday
School Class taught by Jim Hess at Peachtree Road United Methodist Church at 9:30 A.M.

505

501) 502) Mailer for a photographer. The inside card pulls out in both directions to complete the name. (USA)
503) Gift from a printer in the form of a slip case containing illustrated selections from famous writers. (USA)
504) Large invitation to an address by Saul Bass on the design of a house style for AT & T. (USA)
505) Poster-size invitation to a Methodist senior Sunday School class. Black and white. (USA)
506) 507) Sheets from a large presentation folder for a maker of air heating equipment. (GER)
508) Cover of a booklet about *Protocol* facilities for the provision of temporary office space in Washington. (USA)

501) 502) Prospekt für einen Photographen. Die innere Karte ist beidseitig herausziehbar zur Ergänzung des Namens. (USA)
503) Geschenkpackung eines Druckers mit illustrierten Beilagen von berühmten Schriftstellern.(USA)
504) Grossformatige Einladung zu einem Vortrag von Saul Bass über die Entwicklung eines Firmen-Signetes. (USA)
505) Einladung in Plakatform zu einer Methodisten-Sonntagsschule für Erwachsene. (USA)
506) 507) Blätter aus einer grossen Prospektmappe für die Firma HY-LO GmbH & Co., Sarstedt. Abb. 506 farbig. (GER)
508) Titelseite einer Broschüre für eine Organisation, die Büroräume in Washington temporär vermietet. (USA)

501) 502) Prospectus d'un photographe. La carte intérieure peut être tirée des deux côtés pour compléter le nom. (USA)
503) Cadeau d'un imprimeur contenant des textes illustrés par des écrivains célèbres. (USA)
504) Invitation à une conférence de Saul Bass sur la mise au point d'une image de marque. (USA)
505) Invitation sous forme d'affiche à une école du dimanche pour adultes. Noir et blanc. (USA)
506) 507) Pages d'un grand prospectus (ill. 506 en couleur) présentant un système de chauffage. (GER)
508) Couverture d'une brochure pour une organisation louant temporairement des bureaux aux hommes d'affaires à Washington. (USA)

507

508

509

511

510

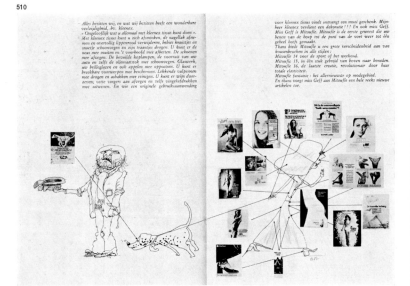

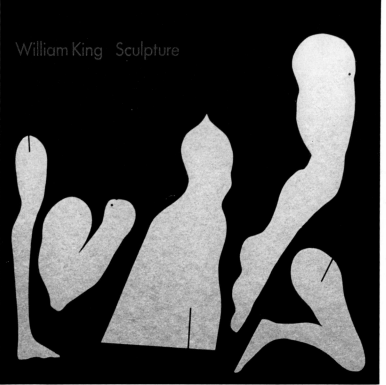

512

513

514

BOING

515

516–523

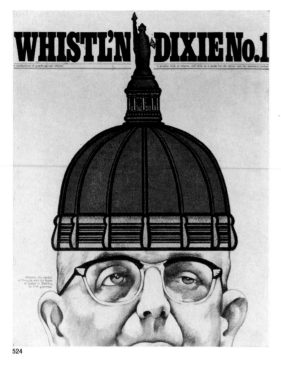

WHISTL'N DIXIE No.1

524

625

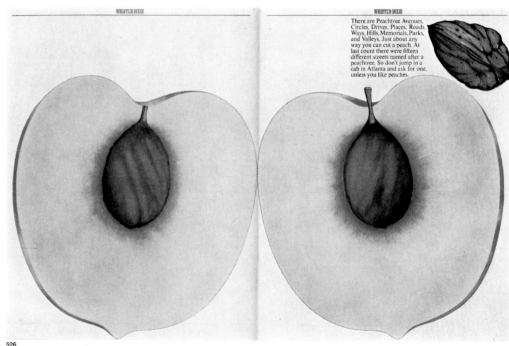

526

524)–526) Cover and double spreads from a newspaper issued by Graphicsgroup, Inc., Atlanta. The cover shows the governor; the gorilla is in the Atlanta zoo; *Coca-Cola* is manufactured locally; and many roads in the area are named after peaches. Four colours. (USA)

527) Double spread from a booklet about the *Filmset* photographic printing technique. (USA)

528) 529) Cover and page from a *Hoechst* booklet from a series, here dealing with immunology. (FRA)

530) Announcement of a programme of environmental studies at York University. White and khaki on deep purple. (USA)

531) Invitation of the National Design Council to an exhibition of home design. Orange and white on blue. (CAN)

532) 533) Mailing envelope and contents furnishing information about kennels for dogs. (USA)

524)–526) Umschlag und Doppelseiten aus einer Publikation eines Graphikerteams in Zeitungsformat. Die Titelseite zeigt den Gouverneur, der Gorilla lebt im städtischen Zoo, *Coca-Cola* wird am Ort produziert und viele Strassen in der Nachbarschaft sind nach Pfirsichen benannt. Vierfarbendruck. (USA)

527) Doppelseite aus einer Broschüre über die *Filmset* Photodruck-Technik. (USA)

528) 529) Umschlag und Seite aus einer *Hoechst*-Broschüre, hier über die Probleme der Immunität. (FRA)

530) Studienprogramm, in Kleinplakatformat, über Umweltfragen für eine Universität. Weiss und Khaki auf Violett. (USA)

531) Einladung der nationalen Beratungsstelle für gute Form zu einer Ausstellung über Innenarchitektur. Orange und weiss auf Blau. (CAN)

532) 533) Versandkuvert und Inhalt über Hunde-«Paläste». (USA)

524)–526) Couverture et doubles pages d'un journal publié par un atelier graphique. La couverture représente le gouverneur de l'Etat, le gorille est un pensionnaire du zoo d'Atlanta, le *Coca-Cola* est fabriqué sur place et plusieurs rues de la ville portent des noms de pêches. (USA)

527) Double page tirée d'une brochure concernant la technique de l'impression photographique *Filmset*. (USA)

528) 529) Couverture et page d'une brochure des Laboratoires *Hoechst*, Paris, traitant de problèmes d'immunité. (FRA)

530) Petite affiche annonçant un programme d'études écologiques dans une université. Polychrome. (USA)

531) Invitation du National Design Council à une exposition de décoration d'intérieurs. Orange et blanc sur bleu. (CAN)

532) 533) Enveloppe et son contenu donnant des informations au sujet de chenils. (USA)

527

Booklets / Prospekte / Prospectus

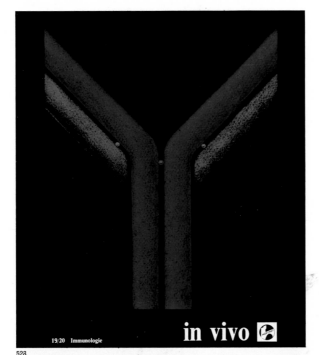

528

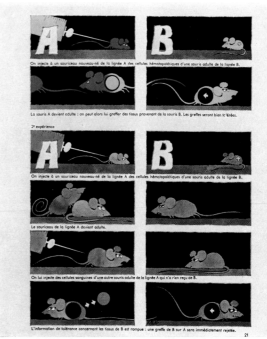

529

530

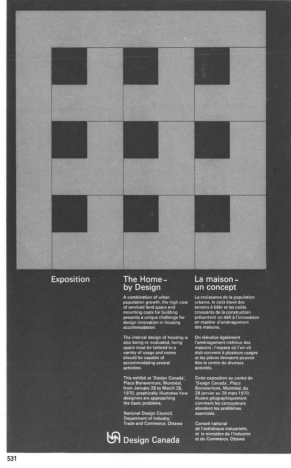

531

532

533

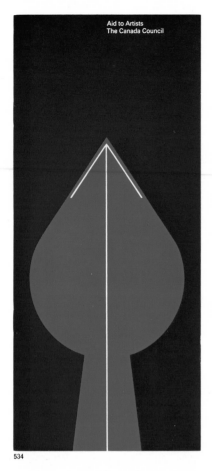

534

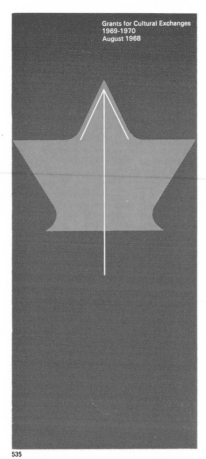

535

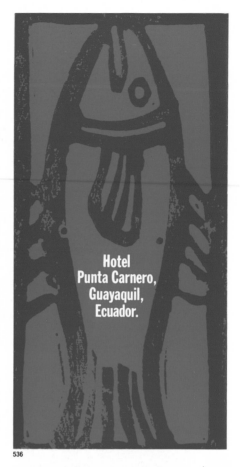

536

537

538

539

534) 535) Covers of brochures from a series about the grants of The Canada Council. (CAN)
536) Cover of a folder about a hotel on the Pacific Coast. (ECU)
537) Cover of a wine list given away to restaurants by Paul Masson Vineyards. Yellow and orange ribbon, olive ground, gold key. (USA)
538) Cover of a folder about a chain of hotels. Four-colour design. (FIN)
539) Concertina-type menu for a restaurant in Paris. Black, white, silver-grey and red. (FRA)
540) 541) Two of ten sheets from a presentation folder announcing the introduction of jumbo jets by *Swissair* in 1971. Black and white. (AUS)
542) Invitation to a champagne supper for the Women's Board of the San Francisco Museum of Art. Dark blue on white. (USA)
543) One side of a folder about a hotel in Hawaii. Full colour. (USA)
544) 545) Double spreads from a booklet about Carnaby Street. Full colour. (GB)

Art Director | Directeur artistique:

534) 535) STUART ASH
536) CLAUDE DIETRICH
537) MICHAEL M. ANDERSON
538) KURT BENGTSSON
539) CHARLES BRIDOUX
542) REIS & MANWARING
543) CLARENCE LEE
544) 545) PETER WINDETT

Agency | Agentur | Agence – Studio:

534) 535) GOTTSCHALK & ASH LTD., MONTREAL
537) JEROME GOULD & ASSOC., LOS ANGELES
539) NOUVELLES GALERIES, PARIS
542) REIS & MANWARING, SAN FRANCISCO
543) CLARENCE LEE DESIGN, HONOLULU
544) 545) JOHN ASTROP LTD., LONDON

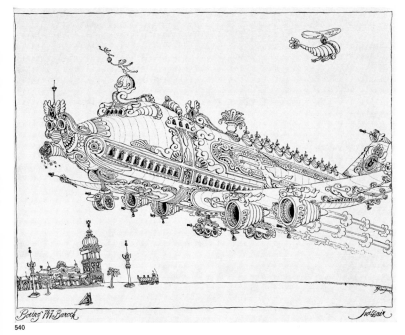

540

541

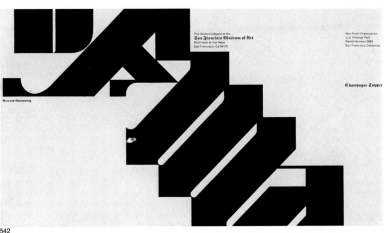

542

543

544

545

534) 535) Umschläge von Prospekten aus einer Serie über Stipendien. (CAN)
536) Umschlag eines Prospektes für ein Hotel an der Pazifischen Küste. (ECU)
537) Umschlag einer Weinliste für Restaurants, herausgegeben von einem Weinbauer. Band gelb und orange, Schlüssel goldfarbig, Grund oliv. (USA)
538) Umschlag eines Faltprospektes mit vierfarbiger Illustration, für eine Hotelkette. (FIN)
539) Ausgestanzte Menukarte in Leporelloform für ein Restaurant in Paris. Schwarz, weiss, silbergrau und rot. (FRA)
540) 541) Zwei von zehn Blättern einer Prospektmappe über die Einführung der Jumbo-Jets im Jahre 1971 durch die *Swissair*. Schwarzweiss. (AUS)
542) Einladung zu einem «Champagner-Bankett» für das Frauenkomitee eines Kunstmuseums. (USA)
543) Aufgeschlagene, ganze Innenseite eines Faltprospektes für ein Hotel in Hawaii. (USA)
544) 545) Mehrfarbige Doppelseiten aus einer Broschüre über die Carnaby Street. (GB)

534) 535) Couvertures de brochures d'une série sur les subventions du The Canada Council. (CAN)
536) Couverture d'un dépliant pour un hôtel sur la côte du Pacifique. (ECU)
537) Couverture d'une carte des vins, distribuée aux restaurants par un viticulteur. Ruban jaune et orange, fond olive, clé dorée. (USA)
538) Couverture d'un dépliant pour une chaîne d'hôtels. Illustration en couleur. (FIN)
539) Menu en accordéon d'un restaurant parisien. Noir, blanc, gris argent et rouge. (FRA)
540) 541) Deux des dix planches d'un portefeuille publicitaire pour la mise en service des jumbo jets par *Swissair* en 1971. Noir et blanc. (AUS)
542) Invitation à un souper au champagne, adressée aux membres d'une association féminine. Bleu foncé sur blanc. (USA)
543) Vue d'un dépliant pour un hôtel de Hawaii. Polychrome. (USA)
544) 545) Doubles pages d'un prospectus sur Carnaby Street, à Londres. Polychrome. (GB)

Annual Reports / Jahresberichte / Rapports Annual

546) Cover of a VSI Corp. annual report. In the plastic enclosure are blind rivets and a poker chip. (USA)
547) Colour cover of a report of Sammons Enterprises, Inc., symbolizing their expanding operations. (USA)
548) Cover of an annual report for Westinghouse Electric Corp. Polychrome figures. (USA)
549) Annual report for Fibreboard Corp. in an integral mailing carton. Green shades. (USA)
550)–552) Two full-page illustrations and a corresponding double spread from an annual report of American Foods, Inc. (USA)
553) 554) Double spreads with full-colour illustrations from an annual report of the Scovill Manufacturing Co., referring to the distribution of sales. (USA)

546) Umschlag eines Jahresberichtes. In der Plastik-Beilage blinde Nieten und Poker-Spielmarke. (USA)
547) Farbiger Umschlag eines Jahresberichtes. Symbolhafte Darstellung der für die Expansion des Unternehmens unternommenen Anstrengungen. (USA)
548) Umschlag eines Jahresberichtes für die Westinghouse Electric Corp. Mehrfarbige Figuren. (USA)
549) Jahresbericht in einem mit dem Bericht fest verbundenen Versandkarton. Grüne Farbtöne. (USA)
550)–552) Zwei ganzseitige Illustrationen und entsprechende Doppelseite aus einem Jahresbericht. (USA)
553) 554) Doppelseiten aus einem Jahresbericht mit mehrfarbigen Illustrationen, die über die Verteilung der getätigten Verkäufe orientieren. (USA)

546) Couverture d'un compte rendu d'exercice. La pochette de plastique y incluse contient des rivets et un jeton de poker. (USA)
547) Couverture polychrome d'un rapport annuel, évoquant symboliquement l'expansion de l'entreprise. (USA)
548) Couverture du compte rendu d'exercice de la Westinghouse Electric Corp. Figures polychromes. (USA)
549) Rapport annuel dans un carton spécialement conçu pour son expédition. Plusieurs tons de vert. (USA)
550)–552) Illustrations sur doubles pages et une de ces pages, tirées du compte rendu d'exercice d'une société d'alimentation. (USA)
553) 554) Doubles pages tirées d'un rapport annuel et évoquant la répartition des ventes. (USA)

446

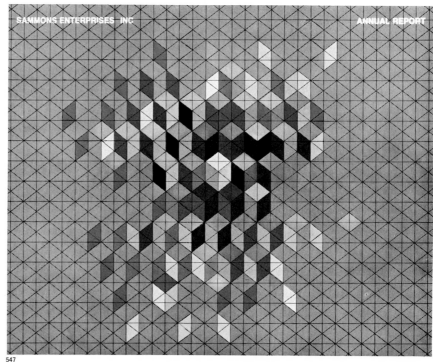

547

548

549

550

552

The Consumer Market: 39% of Sales

Scovill is a Hamilton Beach electric knife or soda fountain drive mixer, a Dominion waffle iron or portable oven, a Haguard or Nylure zipper, a Gripper snap fastener, a Dritz electric scissors or sewing basket, a Clinton safety pin. Scovill is a container of cosmetics, a spray of deodorant, Scovill is a Bagene garment bag, a Gem paper clip, a Hero knitting needle. Scovill is all of these things—and many more—that help to make our daily lives more convenient and more comfortable.

553

The Automotive Market: 14% of Sales

There's no car called a Scovill, but every car has some Scovill in it. We continue to make fine valves and grille parts and dashboards and radiator parts, including the brakes that help cars keep their cool. But we are placing increasing emphasis on the development and production of the systems approach to the automotive business—such products as air conditioning hose assemblies, emission control systems to reduce pollution, and, in the future, air control devices that can power your car's accessories. All of this means more Scovill growth in this important automotive market, regardless of how many cars Detroit builds in any one year. No, there's no Scovill Super Deluxe V-8, but without Scovill parts and systems there wouldn't be any other Super Deluxe.

554

551

Artist | Künstler | Artiste:

546) KEITH BRIGHT & ASSOC.
547) JERRY HERRING
548) PAUL RAND
549) STAN SOLLID/RONALD RAMPLEY
550)–552) THE BROTHERS BOGUSKY
553) 554) VIN GIULIANI/LES SEGAL

Art Director | Directeur artistique:

546) KEITH BRIGHT
547) JERRY HERRING
548) PAUL RAND
549) RONALD RAMPLEY
553) 554) LES SEGAL

Agency | Agentur | Agence – Studio:

547) GLENN ADVERTISING/
STAN RICHARDS & ASSOC., DALLAS
549) LOGAN, CAREY & REHAG, SAN FRANCISCO
550)–552) M/H/S, INC.,
553) 554) CORPORATE ANNUAL REPORTS, INC., N.Y.

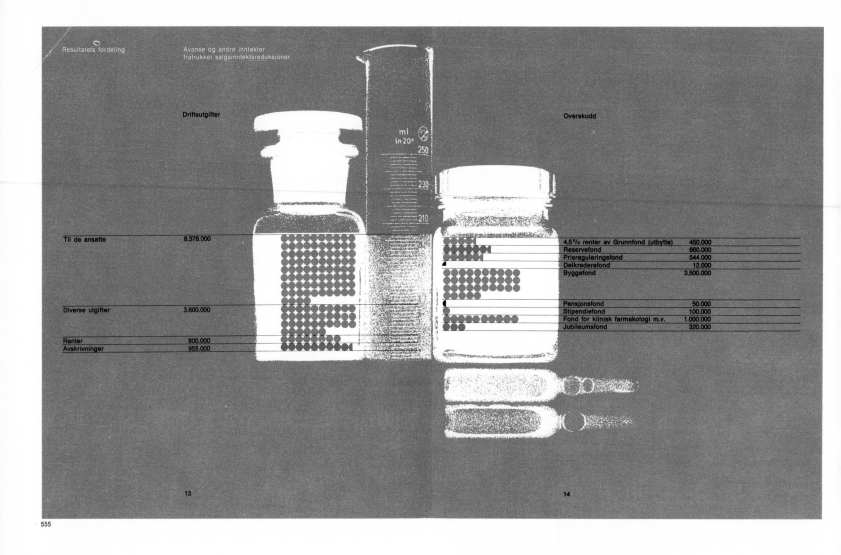

Driftsutgifter

Overskudd

ml
in 20°
250

230

210

Til de ansatte	8.378.000	4,5 % renter av Grunnfond (utbytte)	450.000
		Reservefond	660.000
		Prisreguleringsfond	544.000
		Delkrederefond	12.000
		Byggefond	3.500.000
Diverse utgifter	3.600.000	Pensjonsfond	50.000
		Stipendiefond	100.000
		Fond for klinisk farmakologi m.v.	1.000.000
		Jubileumsfond	320.000
Renter	800.000		
Avskrivninger	955.000		

13

14

555

555) 557) 558) Double spreads from an annual report for Norsk Medisinaldepot, a pharmaceutical company. Numerical data are combined with graphic motifs in colour. (NOR)
556) Cover illustration for an annual report of Restaurant Associates Industries, Inc. (USA)
559) 561) Cover in muted colours and full-page black-and-white illustration from an annual report of the Perfect Film & Chemical Corp., which operates in the photo-finishing and publishing areas. (USA)
560) Full-page illustration from an annual report of the VSI Corporation, which is active in the aerospace industry. Polychrome on blue ground. (USA)

555) 557) 558) Doppelseiten aus dem Jahresbericht eines Unternehmens der pharmazeutischen Branche. Die numerischen Daten sind durch farbige, graphische Motive untermalt. (NOR)
556) Illustration eines Umschlages für den Jahresbericht einer Kette von Restaurants. (USA)
559) 561) Umschlag in matten Farben und ganzseitige, schwarzweisse Illustration aus dem Jahresbericht eines Unternehmens, das sich auf photographischem und verlegerische.n Gebiet spezialisiert. (USA)
560) Ganzseitige Illustration aus einem Jahresbericht für ein in der Raumfahrtindustrie tätiges Unternehmen. Mehrfarbig auf blauem Grund. (USA)

555) 557) 558) Doubles pages du rapport annuel d'un laboratoire pharmaceutique. Les données numériques sont combinées avec des motifs graphiques en couleur. (NOR)
556) Illustration pour la couverture du rapport annuel d'une chaîne de restaurants. (USA)
559) 561) Couverture (teintes passées) et illustration (page entière en noir et blanc) du compte rendu d'exercice d'une entreprise spécialisée dans les montages et l'édition photographiques. (USA)
560) Page tirée du rapport annuel d'une société dont les activités sont liées à l'industrie spatiale. Illustration en couleur sur fond bleu. (USA)

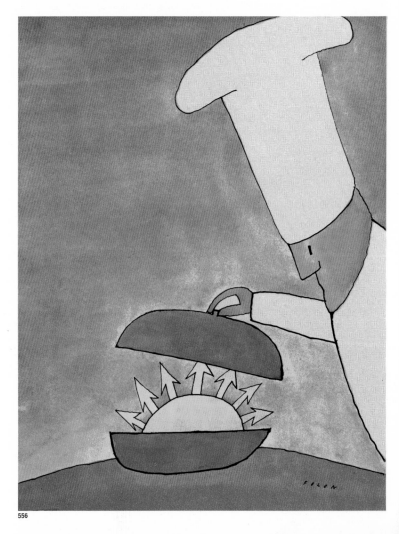

556

**Annual Reports / Jahresberichte
Rapports Annuels**

563

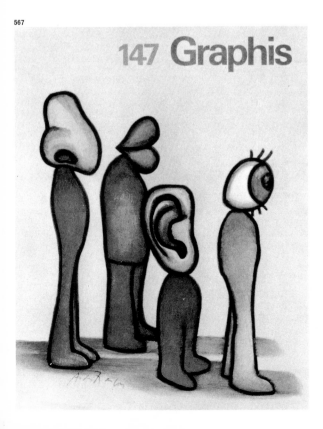

567

147 Graphis

562) Cover of the bi-monthly graphic design magazine LINEA GRAFICA. Black on silver. (ITA)
563) Complete cover of AMERYKA, the Polish edition of an official magazine about America, here on whether television shows reality. (USA)
564)–566) Covers of PHILOBIBLON, a quarterly for collectors of books and graphic art. Black and red on ivory. (GER)
567) Cover of the magazine GRAPHIS. Coloured figures representing the senses on white ground. (SWI)

562) Umschlag einer Ausgabe der Zweimonatszeitschrift für graphische Gestaltung LINEA GRAFICA. Schwarz auf Silber. (ITA)
563) Vollständiger Umschlag einer Nummer von AMERYKA, der polnischen Ausgabe einer offiziellen Zeitschrift über Amerika, hier darüber, ob das Fernsehen tatsächlich die Wirklichkeit zeigt. (USA)
564)–566) Drei Umschläge der Vierteljahresschrift PHILOBIBLON. (GER)
567) Umschlag einer Ausgabe der Zeitschrift GRAPHIS. Die farbigen Figuren stellen die Sinne dar. (SWI)

562) Couverture de la revue bimestrielle d'art graphique LINEA GRAFICA. Noir sur argent. (ITA)
563) Vue de la couverture de AMERYKA, l'édition polonaise d'une revue officielle consacrée à l'Amérique. (USA)
564)–566) Couvertures de PHILOBIBLON, revue trimestrielle destinée aux collectionneurs de livres et d'art graphique. (GER)
567) Couverture de la revue GRAPHIS. Figures polychromes, évoquant les sens, sur fond blanc. (SWI)

**Magazine Covers / Zeitschriften-Umschläge
Couvertures de périodiques**

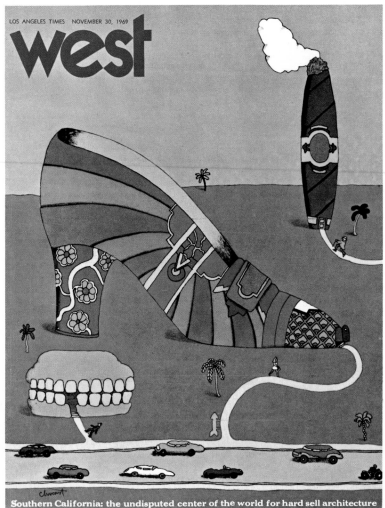

Southern California: the undisputed center of the world for hard sell architecture

568

L.A.'S RECORDING GAME ON A PLATTER

569

KNOW YOUR LOCAL NEWSCASTER
SWINGING IN MANHATTAN BEACH
THE SECRET SIDE OF JUAN MARICHAL

571

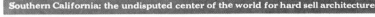

572

587

588

Artist / Künstler / Artiste:

587) MACIEJ ŹBIBOWSKI
588) 591) ANDRZEJ KRAJEWSKI
589) 590) ROMAN CIESLEWICZ
592) VIN GIULIANI/RICHARD HESS
593) GILBERT STONE/MICHAEL RAND
594) MARIAN STACHURSKI

Art Director / Directeur artistique:

587)–591) LECH ZAHORSKI
592) RICHARD HESS
593) MICHAEL RAND

Agency / Agentur / Agence – Studio:

587)–591) INTERPRESS AGENCE POLONAISE, WARSAW
592) HESS AND/OR ANTUPIT, NEW YORK

Publisher / Verleger / Editeur:

587)–591) POLONIA VERLAG, WARSAW
592) U.N. ASSOCIATION, NEW YORK
593) THE SUNDAY TIMES, LONDON
594) PROJEKT, WARSAW

Magazine Covers
Zeitschriften-Umschläge
Couvertures de périodiques

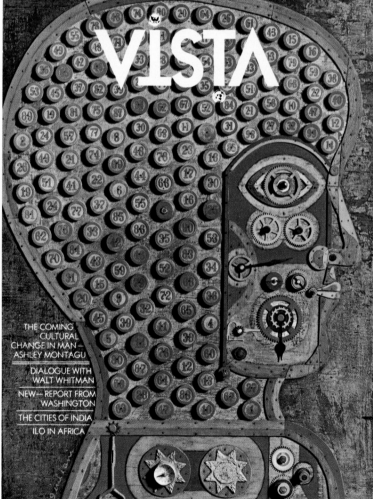

592

587)–591) Front and complete covers of the monthly magazine POLAND devoted to modern cultural life in Poland, which appears in six languages. Titles of the covers: 587 'Transience'; 588 'Three Men'; 589 'To Those on the High Seas'. (POL)

592) Cover of the bi-monthly magazine VISTA, a publication of the United Nations Association, here illustrating 'the coming cultural change in man'. (USA)

593) Cover of THE SUNDAY TIMES magazine, here containing a feature on famous scandal stories. Brown and green figures on turquoise and lavender. (GB)

594) Cover of the design magazine PROJEKT. Bright colours between torn edges. (POL)

587)–591) Titelseiten und vollständige Umschläge der Monatszeitschrift POLEN, die dem kulturellen Leben des modernen Polens gewidmet ist und in sechs Sprachen herausgegeben wird. Die Titel der gezeigten Umschläge: Abb. 587 «Vergänglichkeit», Abb. 588: «Drei Männer», Abb. 589: «Den Männern auf See gewidmet». (POL)

592) Umschlag der Zweimonatszeitschrift VISTA, einer Publikation der Vereinten Nationen, hier über «die zukünftige kulturelle Wandlung in der menschlichen Gesellschaft». (USA)

593) Umschlag der Zeitschrift THE SUNDAY TIMES, hier mit einem Artikel über berühmte Skandalgeschichten. Gestalten in Braun und Grün auf türkisblauem und violettem Grund. (GB)

594) Umschlag der Zeitschrift PROJEKT. Lebhafte Farben zwischen angerissenen Rändern. (POL)

587)–591) Plats et vues entières de couvertures de la revue mensuelle POLOGNE, consacrée à la vie culturelle contemporaine en Pologne et publiée en six langues. Titres des couvertures: 587 «Transience», 588 «Trois hommes»; 589 «Pour ceux qui sont en mer». (POL)

592) Couverture de la revue bimestrielle VISTA, une publication des Nations Unies illustrant ici «l'avènement d'une nouvelle société culturelle». (USA)

593) Couverture d'un numéro du SUNDAY TIMES MAGAZINE contenant un article sur les histoires à scandale célèbres. Figures en brun et vert sur turquoise et lavande. (GB)

594) Couverture de la revue graphique PROJEKT. Couleurs vives entre bords déchirés. (POL)

590

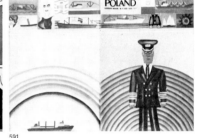

591

589

593

594

595

596

598

599

595) Cover of KONTAKT, a magazine for young people, here with an article on cybernetics. Blue and black. (SWI)

596) Cover of an issue of NEW YORK magazine containing an article on Nelson Rockefeller. (USA)

597) Cover of DOMUS, a magazine of architecture and interior design. Black and white, yellow ring and title. (ITA)

598) Cover of an issue of the monthly TRENTE JOURS containing a feature on two *bon vivants*. Full colour. (SWI)

599)–602) Covers of TIME magazine. The subjects are Negro problems, the 'middle Americans' and the candidates for the mayoralty of New York. (USA)

595) Umschlag einer Nummer von KONTAKT, einer Zeitschrift für junge Menschen, hier mit einem Artikel über Kybernetik. (SWI)

596) Umschlag einer Ausgabe der Zeitschrift NEW YORK. Die Illustration bezieht sich auf einen Artikel über Nelson Rockefeller. (USA)

597) Umschlag der Zeitschrift DOMUS, einer Publikation für Architektur und Innendekoration. Schwarzweiss, Ring und Titel gelb. (ITA)

598) Umschlag einer Ausgabe der Monatsschrift TRENTE JOURS, mit einem Artikel über «Zwei Ritter vom guten Leben». (SWI)

599)–602) Umschläge der Zeitschrift TIME, hier über die Negerprobleme, den «durchschnittlichen» Amerikaner und die Kandidaten für das Amt des Bürgermeisters von New York. (USA)

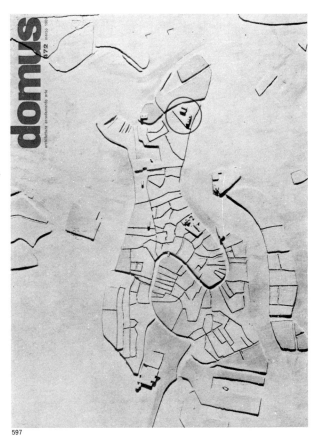

597

601

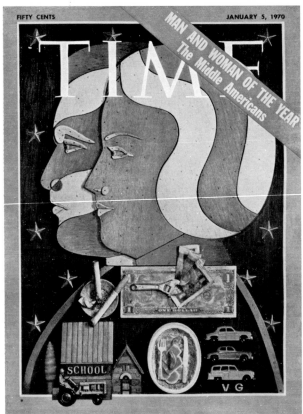

600

602

595) Couverture de KONTAKT, une revue destinée aux jeunes et contenant. ici, un article sur la cybernétique. Bleu et noir. (SWI)
596) Couverture d'un numéro de la revue NEW YORK contenant un article sur Nelson Rockefeller. (USA)
597) Couverture de DOMUS, revue d'architecture et de décoration. Noir et blanc, cercle et titre en jaune. (ITA)
598) Couverture d'un numéro de la revue mensuelle TRENTE JOURS contenant un article sur deux bons vivants. Polychrome. (SWI)
599)–602) Couverture de l'hebdomadaire TIME. Les sujets en sont le problème des Noirs, les «Américains moyens» et les candidats à la mairie de New York. (USA)

175

603

Publisher | Verleger | Editeur:

603)–605) 607) PRINT MAGAZINE, NEW YORK
606) ONTARIO DEPT. OF LABOUR, ONTARIO
608)–611) NATIONAL FEDERATION OF LICENSED PRACTICAL NURSES, NEW YORK

604

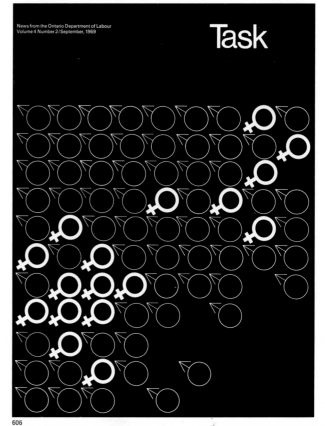

606

Artist | Künstler | Artiste

603) JOSÉ PLA NARBONA
604) RICHARD HESS
605) JEAN MICHEL FOLON
606) WILLIAM NEWTON/BILL HEDGES
607) PETER CAMPBELL
608) 610) 611) CHARLES GOSLIN
609) DAVID BARNETT

Art Director | Directeur artistique:

603)–605) 607) ANDREW KNER
606) WILLIAM NEWTON
608)–611) SIDNEY MILLER

Agency | Agentur | Agence – Studio:

606) NEWTON PUBLISHING LTD., TORONTO
608)–611) GOSLIN/BARNETT, BROOKLYN, N.Y.

**Magazine Covers / Zeitschriften-Umschläge
Couvertures de périodiques**

608

609

605

610

611

607

603)–605) 607) Covers of the bi-monthly graphic design magazine PRINT. Fig. 604 refers to 'magazines after McLuhan', fig. 605 to 'signs and symbols'. (USA)

606) Cover of TASK, a magazine published by the Ontario Department of Labour. The reference is to women in the labour force. White on dull orange. (CAN)

608)–611) Covers of the monthly magazine BEDSIDE NURSE. Black and one colour. (USA)

603)–605) 607) Umschläge der zweimonatlich erscheinenden Zeitschrift für Graphik PRINT. Abb. 604 bezieht sich auf «Zeitschriften nach McLuhan», Abb. 605 auf «Zeichen und Symbole». (USA)

606) Umschlag einer Ausgabe von TASK, einer Zeitschrift, die vom Arbeitsamt in Ontario herausgegeben wird. Die Zeichnung illustriert das Thema «Frauen im Arbeitsprozess». Weiss auf stumpfem Orange. (CAN)

608)–611) Umschläge von vier Nummern der Monatszeitschrift BEDSIDE NURSE. (USA)

603)–605) 607) Couvertures de la revue bimestrielle d'art graphique PRINT. L'ill. 604 évoque «les revues après McLuhan», 605 «les signes et les symboles». (USA)

606) Couverture de TASK, une revue publiée par le Département du travail de l'Ontario. L'illustration évoque la place des femmes au sein des forces ouvrières. Blanc sur orange. (CAN)

608)–611) Couvertures de la revue mensuelle BEDSIDE NURSE. Noir et une couleur. (USA)

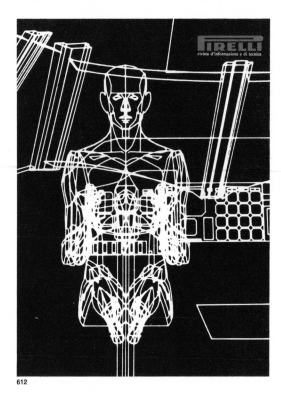

612

for 30,000 tons of frozen watermelon. P.S. What are you doing about our silver mine in Nevada? I hear it's tarnishing."

Blade is now a milkman in Denver, and he is said to be recovering very nicely. But he may have to quit his job. The dairy he works for is considering diversifying its business by adding egg nog.

The more diversified a company gets, the more difficult it becomes to maintain a distinctive corporate image. For instance, a few years ago Peerless Pigskin Corp. had no identity problem. Its slogan, "Pigskins Are Our Proudest Product," was known around the world. But then, in rapid succession, Peerless went into pickles, plastics and pontoon bridges. The slogan became dated, and Wall Street rumors had it that investors were shying away from Peerless because they simply weren't sure what the company was any longer.

Parker Peerless, founder and chairman, took the problem to the company's advertising agency, Chilblains & Fever: "Look," he said, "if you want to keep our account, you've got to come up with a new image for us. Pigskins, pickles, plastics and pontoon bridges are not so complicated,

so get with it. And let's have something catchy, right?"

The agency put its top creative man on the job. After two months of mind-bending exertion, he came up with a winning combination of words. Staggering into the office of the agency head, he was about to deliver his gem when the Peerless account man came bursting in. "Hold it," the account executive screamed. "Peerless has just gone into pajamas!"

Back at his desk, the creative had barely begun to try fitting pajamas into the picture when the creative director popped into his office. "By the way," he said casually, "Peerless just signed to acquire Proudfoot Paints. Try to slip a mention of paints into what you're doing, won't you? That's a good lad."

And every time that the agency would come up with a new corporate image, Peerless would go into a new line: perambulators, percolators, poultry, polyethylene. Finally, the creative man ran off to join the Green Berets, Chilblains & Fever lost the account, and Peerless never managed a good public image. But it really didn't matter. Shortly thereafter, Peerless was acquired by Posito's Pizza,

and it became Posito's problem.

Conglomerates do not hesitate to cross cultural, ethnic and geographic lines. One of the problems that can arise out of this is a language gap. When Go Go Corp., a fast-growing Yankee company, acquired Boll Weevil Mills, a slow-growing but profitable operation, it appeared to be a good deal for everyone concerned. Boll Weevil was knee-deep in crack salesmen at its headquarters, just a spare-rib's throw from Fatback, Ark., and Go Go needed skilled sales help badly.

So it was that Beauregard Bixbee, top salesman for Boll Weevil, was summarily transferred to the New York office of Go Go, promoted, given a lavish raise and turned loose on the Eastern market. Alas, the move was a disaster.

Though suave to a fault, Bixbee was an adherent of the "You-get-more-sales-with-honey-than-vinegar" school. He would drift lazily up to the receptionist and intone softly, "Pard'n me, honey, but mah goodness if you all haven't got the purtiest little ol' blue eyes in the ever-lovin' world, cross mah palpitatin' heart. You all think your fine old boss could spare a poor country boy a few minutes of his time?"

613

615

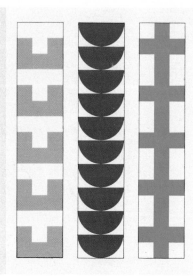

616

Banners, traditionally one of the most exciting forms of public art, are also the most eloquent spokesmen of the human condition. Like man himself, the banner is both rooted to the earth and inclined freely toward the heavens.
Banners express the continual dynamic between physical and spiritual. Grounded, they float free in kinetic excitement from their point of static mooring.

Center designers created a series of banners for Chicago's Civic Center Plaza. They transform the plaza into a multi-use environment, humanizing the seat of government, converting a neutral expanse of steel, stone, and glass into a fanciful playground. The banners soar with the wind, evolving a litany of shapes, carving out of the sky the aspirations of a city self-consciously in quest of its destiny.
Chicago's banners celebrate the loftiness of human ambition, grounded in human experience. The proud declarative, "I Will," billows with each gust that sweeps the Civic Center Plaza.

Artist | Künstler | Artiste:

612) PINO TOVAGLIA
613) GIUSEPPE LUCCI/MARTIN PEDERSON
614) CLARENCE TAYLOR/PHIL JORDAN
615) MICHAEL FOREMAN
616) ORLANDO CABANBAN/GIULIO CITTATO
617) KOHEI SUGIURA

Art Director | Directeur artistique:

612) PINO TOVAGLIA/TERESITA CAMAGNI-HANGELDIAN
613) MARTIN PEDERSON
614) PHIL JORDAN
615) DEREK BIRDSALL
616) GIULIO CITTATO
617) KOHEI SUGIURA

Agency | Agentur | Agence – Studio:

612) CENTRO S.R.L., MILAN
613) GARDNER ADVERTISING COMPANY, INC., NEW YORK
614) BEVERIDGE & ASSOCIATES, INC., WASHINGTON, D.C.
615) OMNIFIC LTD., LONDON

Publisher | Verleger | Editeur:

612) PIRELLI S.P.A., MILAN
613) AMERICAN AIRLINES, NEW YORK
614) CONSTRUCTION SPECIFICATIONS INSTITUTE, WASHINGTON, D.C.
615) MOBIL OIL CO. LTD., LONDON
616) CENTER FOR ADVANCED RESEARCH IN DESIGN, CHICAGO
617) SHISEIDO CO. LTD., TOKYO

House Organs / Hauszeitschriften
Journaux d'entreprises

648

651

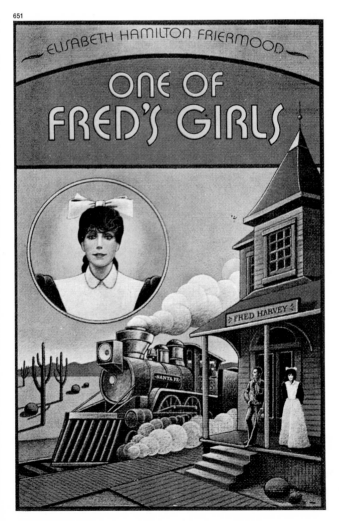

652

Art Director | Directeur artistique:

646) REINHARD KLEIN
648) NICHOLAS THIRKELL
649) 650) ETIENNE DELESSERT
651) JIM DAVIS
652) JOSÉ PLA NARBONA

Agency | Agentur | Agence – Studio:

648) NICHOLAS THIRKELL ASSOC., LONDON
652) STUDIO PLA NARBONA, BARCELONA

Publisher | Verleger | Editeur:

646) HERDER VERLAG, FREIBURG/GER
647) WEIDENFELD & NICHOLSON PUBLISHING, LONDON
648) MACMILLAN & CO. LTD., LONDON
649) 650) LE LIVRE DU MOIS, LAUSANNE
651) DOUBLEDAY & CO., INC., NEW YORK
652) EDICIONES ALFAGUARA S.A., MADRID

653

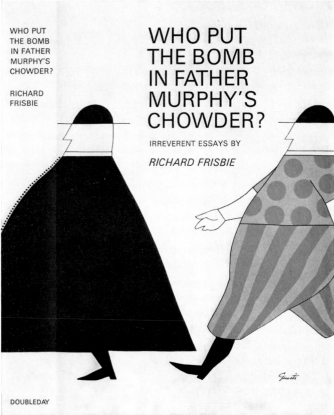

654

655

658

653) Spine and front cover of a book of wedding poems. Illustration in bright colours, pink ground. Laminated. (GB)
654) Spine and front cover of a book of 'irreverent' essays. Black and two reds. (USA)
655) Cover of a sociological work (Our Lost Ego). Ochre, red and black, white lettering. (SWI)
656) Jacket of a detective novel (Sjutton Kills Birds). Pen drawing, black and red. (SWE)
657) Jacket of a collection of stories about robbers. Green, black and red, laminated. (GER)
658) 659) Covers from an educational series of plays for reading. Yellow/black and mustard/black. (USA)
660) Cover of a book about 'dragons, snakes and monsters'. Polychrome illustration, laminated. (GER)

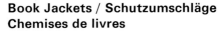

Book Jackets / Schutzumschläge
Chemises de livres

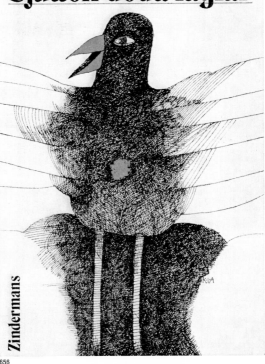

656

659

657

660

Artist | Künstler | Artiste:

653) PETER BENTLEY
654) GEORGE GIUSTI
655) PETER RÜFENACHT-BOLLI
656) KJELL IVAN ANDERSON
657) GÜNTHER STILLER
658) 659) STEPHEN OSBORN
660) WALTER GRIEDER

Art Director | Directeur artistique:

653) NICHOLAS THIRKELL
655) PETER RÜFENACHT-BOLLI
658) 659) BARBARA LINDSLEY
660) WERNER SKAMBRAKS/WALTER GRIEDER

Agency | Agentur | Agence – Studio:

653) BENTLEY/FARRELL/BURNETT, LONDON
658) 659) STEPHEN OSBORN & ASSOC.,
          PALO ALTO, CALIF.

Publisher | Verleger | Editeur:

653) MACMILLAN & CO., LTD., LONDON
654) DOUBLEDAY & CO., INC., NEW YORK
655) ARTEMIS VERLAG, ZÜRICH
656) ZINDERMANS FÖRLAG, GÖTEBORG/SWE
657) EUGEN DIEDERICHS VERLAG,
          DÜSSELDORF
658) 659) EDUCATIONAL DEVELOPMENT
          CORP., PALO ALTO, CALIF.
660) LOEWES VERLAG, BAYREUTH/GER

653) Rücken und Vorderseite eines Buchumschlages für eine Sammlung von Hochzeitsgedichten. Illustration in lebhaften Farben auf rosa Grund. Umschlag laminiert. (GB)

654) Rücken und Vorderseite eines Umschlages für ein Buch mit «respektlosen» Essays. Schwarz und zwei Rottöne. (USA)

655) Umschlag für ein soziologisches Werk. Ocker, rot und schwarz, Text in Weiss. (SWI)

656) Umschlag eines Kriminalromans (Sjutton tötet Vögel). Federzeichnung in Schwarz und Rot. (SWE)

657) Laminierter Buchumschlag für eine Sammlung von Räubergeschichten. Grün, schwarz und rot. (GER)

658) 659) Zweifarbige Buchumschläge zweier Bücher aus einer Serie von Theaterstücken zum Vorlesen. (USA)

660) Laminierter, mehrfarbiger Buchumschlag. (GER)

653) Dos et plat de la couverture laminée d'un recueil de poèmes nuptiaux. Illustration de couleurs vives sur fond rose. (GB)

654) Dos et plat de la couverture d'un recueil d'essais «irrévérencieux». Noir et deux tons de rouge. (USA)

655) Couverture d'un ouvrage de sociologie. Ocre, rouge et noir, texte en blanc. (SWI)

656) Chemise d'un roman policier (Sjutton tue les oiseaux). Dessin à la plume en noir et rouge. (SWE)

657) Chemise laminée d'un recueil d'histoires de brigands. Vert, noir et rouge. (GER)

658) 659) Couvertures d'ouvrages parus dans une collection éducative de pièces de théâtre. Jaune/noir et moutarde/noir. (USA)

660) Couverture laminée d'un livre consacré «aux dragons, aux serpents et aux monstres». Illustration en couleur. (GER)

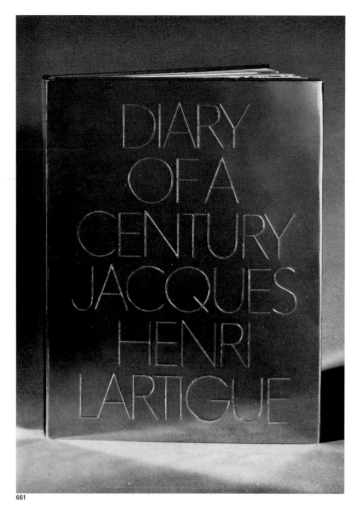

661

Das Märchenbuch der Welt

Diederichs

662

Alphabet Book

664

The Magic of English Workbook

Beginning Experiences in English as a Second Language

Name

Teacher's Edition

665

663

Artist | Künstler | Artiste:

661) BEA FEITLER
662) WILFRIED BLECHER
663) HEINRICH HUSSMANN
664) 665) CARL KOCK/JAMES A. BUDDENBAUM
666) 667) EDWARD SOREL

Art Director | Directeur artistique:

661) BEA FEITLER
663) HEINRICH HUSSMANN
664) 665) JAMES A. BUDDENBAUM
666) 667) GEORGES MCHARGUE

Publisher | Verleger | Editeur:

661) THE VIKING PRESS, INC., NEW YORK
662) EUGEN DIEDERICHS VERLAG, DÜSSELDORF
663) GUIDO PRESSLER VERLAG, WIESBADEN
664) 665) HARPER & ROW, PUBLISHERS, INC., NEW YORK
666) 667) DOUBLEDAY & CO., INC., NEW YORK

661) Dust jacket for a photographic survey of the life of J. H. Lartigue. Blind embossing on gold foil. (USA)
662) Jacket of a collection of fairy tales. Colour illustration. (GER)
663) Cover of a book about books. Red, white and black. (GER)
664) 665) Covers of two children's workbooks for the teaching of English. Four colours. (USA)
666) 667) Complete cover, and detail of the drawing, for an illustrated story of a duck. (USA)

661) Buchumschlag für eine photographische Übersicht über unser Jahrhundert. Blindprägung auf Goldfolie. (USA)
662) Mehrfarbiger Buchumschlag für eine Sammlung von Märchen aus aller Welt. (GER)
663) Bunter Umschlag für eine Abhandlung über Bücher. (GER)
664) 665) Vierfarbige Umschläge zweier Lehrbücher für Englisch. (USA)
666) 667) Vollständiger Umschlag und Detail der Zeichnung für eine illustrierte Geschichte über eine Ente. (USA)

661) Chemise d'un répertoire photographique du siècle. Gaufrage à sec sur feuille d'or. (USA)
662) Chemise polychrome d'un recueil de légendes du monde entier. (GER)
663) Couverture d'un traité sur les livres. Polychrome. (GER)
664) 665) Couvertures de deux manuels scolaires pour l'enseignement de l'anglais. Quatre couleurs. (USA)
666) 667) Couverture et détail de l'illustration, pour l'histoire illustrée d'un canard. (USA)

666

667

668

669

671

672

Artist | Künstler | Artiste:

668)–670) WALTER GRIEDER
671) FLAVIO COSTANTINI
672) RALPH STEADMAN
673) JERZY FLISAK
674) MICHAEL FOREMAN

Art Director | Directeur artistique:

668)–670) WALTER GRIEDER
672) DENNIS DOBSON
673) ANDRZEJ HEIDRICH
674) MICHAEL BROWN

Publisher | Verleger | Editeur:

668) JOYCE-BOOKS AG, BASEL
669) DIOGENES VERLAG AG, ZÜRICH
670) BENZIGER VERLAG, ZÜRICH
671) DOBSON BOOKS LTD., LONDON/EMME EDIZIONI, MILAN
672) DOBSON BOOKS LTD., LONDON
673) CZYTELNIK, WARSAW
674) HAMISH HAMILTON LTD., LONDON

670

668) Cover of a large-format children's book (The Visit to the Factory). (SWI)
669) Cover of a children's book (Silverleg the Great). Full colour. (SWI)
670) Full-colour jacket of a children's book (Willy and the Flying Tram). (SWI)
671) Large-format cover in full colour for an English adaptation of a poem by Mayakovsky about a toy horse. (GB)
672) Complete jacket for a children's book about a train driver. Full colour. (GB)
673) Jacket of a children's book of peasant tales. Yellow, green, rust and black on rose madder ground. (POL)
674) Jacket of a children's book about a hippopotamus who went out to see the world. Full colour. (GB)

668) Umschlag eines grossformatigen Kinderbuches. (SWI)
669) Mehrfarbiger Umschlag eines Kinderbuches. (SWI)
670) Umschlag in lebhaften Farben für ein Kinderbuch. (SWI)
671) Umschlag für ein grossformatiges Kinderbuch, in dem ein Gedicht von Majakowski über ein Spielzeug-Pferd neu erzählt wird. Kräftige Farben. (GB)
672) Vollständiger Umschlag für ein Kinderbuch über einen Lokomotivführer. (GB)
673) Vollständiger Umschlag eines Kinderbuches mit Bauerngeschichten. Gelb, grün, rostfarbig und schwarz auf blassem Rosa-Grund. (POL)
674) Mehrfarbiger Umschlag eines Kinderbuches über die Geschichte eines Nilpferdes, das auf Reisen ging, um die Welt kennenzulernen. (GB)

668) Couverture grand format d'un livre d'enfants (La visite à l'usine). (SWI)
669) Couverture d'un livre d'enfants. Polychrome. (SWI)
670) Chemise polychrome d'un livre d'enfants (Willy et le tram volant). (SWI)
671) Couverture grand format de l'adaptation en anglais d'un poème de Mayakovsky, inspiré par un cheval de bois. Polychrome. (GB)
672) Chemise d'un livre d'enfants racontant l'histoire d'un chauffeur de locomotive. Polychrome. (GB)
673) Chemise d'un recueil d'histoires paysannes pour les enfants. Jaune, vert, rouille et noir sur fond rose pâle. (POL)
674) Chemise d'un livre d'enfants racontant l'histoire d'un hippopotame qui partit à la découverte du monde. Polychrome. (GB)

673

674

675

676

677

678

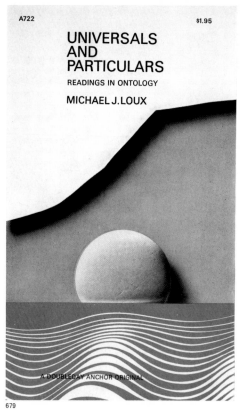

679

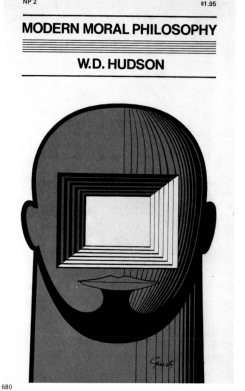

680

675) Cover of a paperback edition of one of Waugh's novels. Four colours. (GB)
676) Cover of a novel. Black and white on blue. (ITA)
677) Cover of a paperback edition of a Remarque novel. Black-and-white figure, blue ground. (ITA)
678) Cover of a paperback. Brown ground. (NLD)
679) Cover of a paperback on ontology. (USA)
680) Cover of a paperback on moral philosophy. Green, blue and black head. (USA)
681) Cover of a paperback about the gospel according to St. Mark. Green and yellow lion. (GER)
682) Cover of a book of stories in a paperback series. Faces in shades of ochre and pink. (GER)
683) Paperback cover for a novel (Confounded Little Baggage). Colour illustration. (GER)
684) Colour cover for a paperback novel. (GER)

675) Umschlag für eine Taschenbuchausgabe. (GB)
676) Romanumschlag. Schwarz und weiss auf Blau. (ITA)
677) Umschlag für einen Roman von Remarque. Schwarz-weisse Figur auf blauem Grund. (ITA)
678) Umschlag aus einer Serie von Kriminalromanen. (NLD)
679) Umschlag eines Taschenbuches mit Vorträgen über Ontologie. Rot, violett und schwarz. (USA)
680) Umschlag eines Buches über moderne Moral-Philosophie. Kopf in Grün, Blau und Schwarz. (USA)
681) Umschlag einer Taschenbuchausgabe des Markus-Evangeliums. Löwe in Grün und Gelb. (GER)
682) Umschlag eines Taschenbuches aus einer Serie mit Erzählungen. Gesichter in Ocker- und Rosatönen. (GER)
683) Umschlag der Taschenbuchausgabe eines Romans. Mehrfarbige Illustration. (GER)
684) Taschenbuchumschlag für einen Roman. (GER)

675) Couverture de l'édition brochée d'un roman d'Evelyn Waugh. Quatre couleurs. (GB)
676) Couverture de roman. Noir et blanc sur bleu. (ITA)
677) Couverture de l'édition brochée d'un roman de Remarque. Figure en noir et blanc sur fond bleu. (ITA)
678) Couverture d'un roman policier. Fond brun. (NLD)
679) Couverture brochée d'un ouvrage d'ontologie. (USA)
680) Couverture d'un ouvrage de poche consacré à la morale moderne. Tête en vert, bleu et noir. (USA)
681) Couverture d'une édition brochée de l'Evangile selon saint Marc. Lion en vert et jaune. (GER)
682) Couverture d'un recueil de nouvelles, paru dans une collection de poche. Visages polychromes. (GER)
683) Couverture brochée d'un roman (Ravissante petite charogne). Illustration en couleur. (GER)
684) Couverture polychrome d'un livre de poche. (GER)

Julius Schniewind
Das Evangelium nach Markus

Siebenstern-Taschenbuch

681

Tina Christian
Verdammtes kleines Luder

rororo

683

Agency | Agentur | Agence – Studio:

675) BENTLEY/FARRELL/BURNETT, LONDON

Publisher | Verleger | Editeur:

675) PENGUIN BOOKS LTD., LONDON
676) PAN, MILAN
677) ARNOLDO MONDADORI EDITORE, MILAN
678) A. W. BRUNA & ZOONS, UTRECHT/NLD
679) 680) DOUBLEDAY & CO., INC., NEW YORK
681) SIEBENSTERN TASCHENBUCH VERLAG, MÜNCHEN
682) FISCHER BÜCHEREI KG, FRANKFURT/M.
683) 684) ROWOHLT TASCHENBUCH VERLAG
GMBH, HAMBURG

Paperbacks / Taschenbücher
Livres brochés

Artist | Künstler | Artiste:

675) PETER BENTLEY
676) RICCARDO MANZI
677) FERNEC PINTÉR
678) DICK BRUNA
679) 680) GEORGE GIUSTI
681)–684) JAN BUCHHOLZ/RENI HINSCH

Art Director | Directeur artistique:

675) DAVID PELHAM
676) RICCARDO MANZI
677) BRUNO BINOSI
678) DICK BRUNA
679) 680) DIANA KLEMIN

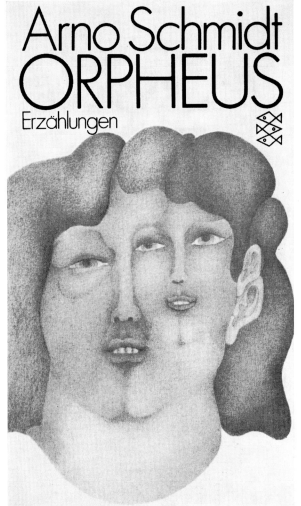

Arno Schmidt
ORPHEUS
Erzählungen

682

A. Pieyre de Mandiargues
Lilie des Meeres

rororo

684

685)–687) Paperback covers from a series of horror stories. Full colour. (USA)
688) Cover of a book of poems. Two greens. (USA)
689) Cover of a paperback novel (The Mill on the Po). (ITA)
690) Cover for a paperback edition of Goldoni's works. (ITA)
691) 692) Paperback covers for novels from a fantastic adventure series. Polychrome. (GB)
693) 694) Illustration and complete cover of a paperback novel based on the imagery of Tarot cards. (USA)

685)–687) Buchumschläge für Greuelgeschichten. (USA)
688) Umschlag für einen Gedichtband (Der zweifache Traum vom Frühling). Zwei Grüntöne. (USA)
689) Romanumschlag (Die Mühle am Po). (ITA)
690) Buchumschlag für Schauspiele von Goldoni. (ITA)
691) 692) Umschläge für Abenteuerromane. (GB)
693) 694) Illustration und ganzer Taschenbuch-Umschlag für einen Roman, der sich mit der Deutung der Kartenbilder eines Tarock-Spieles befasst. (USA)

685)–687) Couvertures polychromes de livres de poche, parus dans une collection d'épouvante. (USA)
688) Couverture d'un recueil de poèmes. (USA)
689) Couverture d'un roman (Le Moulin du Pò). (ITA)
690) Couverture de l'édition brochée d'un recueil de pièces de Goldoni. (ITA)
691) 692) Couvertures de romans d'aventure. (GB)
693) 694) Illustration et couverture brochée d'un roman inspiré par les tarots. (USA)

685

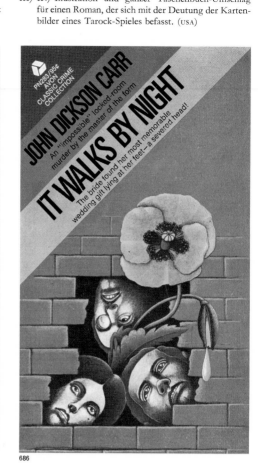

686

687

689

690

691

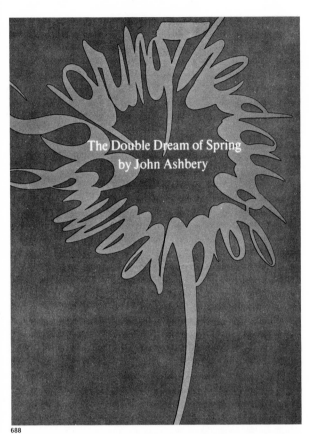

688

693

692

694

Artist | Künstler | Artiste:

685)–687) ROGER HANE/BARBARA BERTOLLI
688) PETER BRADFORD
689) FERENC PINTÉR
690) PAOLO GUIDOTTI
691 692) ROGER HANE
693) 694) GILBERT STONE/BARBARA BERTOLLI

Art Director | Directeur artistique:

685)–687) 693) 694) BARBARA BERTOLLI
688) ALBERT CETTA
689) 690) BRUNO BINOSI
691) 692) AVA WEISS

Agency | Agentur | Agence – Studio:

688) PETER BRADFORD & ASSOC., NEW YORK

Publisher | Verleger | Editeur:

685)–687) 693) 694) AVON BOOKS, NEW YORK
688) E. P. DUTTON COMPANY, NEW YORK
689) 690) ARNOLDO MONDADORI EDITORE, MILAN
691) 692) COLLIER BOOKS, NEW YORK

Paperbacks
Taschenbücher
Livres brochés

695

696

699

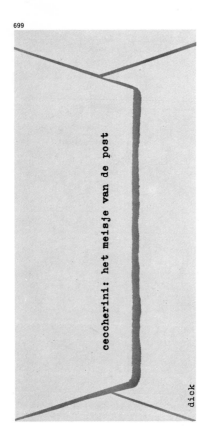

700

Agency | Agentur | Agence – Studio:

695) 696) PETER MAX ENTERPRISES, NEW YORK
697) BENTLEY/FARRELL/BURNETT, LONDON
701) 702) STUDIO GÖRANSSON & CO., STOCKHOLM

Publisher | Verleger | Editeur:

695) 696) WILLIAM MORROW & CO., INC., NEW YORK
697) WEIDENFELD & NICOLSON, LONDON
698) MICHAEL JOSEPH LTD., LONDON
699) A. W. BRUNA & ZOONS PUBLISHERS, UTRECHT/NLD
700) CRV, LAUSANNE
701) 702) FORUM AB, STOCKHOLM
703) SIMON & SCHUSTER, INC., NEW YORK

721

722

725

Artist | Künstler | Artiste:

719) PAUL DAVIS
720) DON WELLER
721) ETIENNE ROBIAL
722) ROBERT WELKER
723) NICK FASCIANO/JOHN BERG
724) STANISLAW ZAGORSKI
725) RICK MEYEROWITZ/TONY LANE

Art Director | Directeur artistique:

719) 723) 725) JOHN BERG
720) JOHN LEPREVOST
721) CLAUDE CAUDRON
722) ROBERT WELKER
724) NESUHI ERTEGUN

Agency | Agentur | Agence – Studio:

720) UNIVERSAL STUDIOS, LOS ANGELES
721) ALAIN MAROUANI, NEUILLY/FRA
722) NADLER & LARIMER, INC., NEW YORK

Publisher | Verleger | Editeur:

719) 723) 725) COLUMBIA RECORDS, NEW YORK
720) UNIVERSAL CITY RECORDS, LOS ANGELES
721) BARCLAY, DISQUES, NEUILLY/FRA
722) KNL MUSIC CORP., NEW YORK
724) ATLANTIC RECORDING CORP., NEW YORK

719) Pochette polychrome pour un enregistrement de pièces récitées par Leadbelly. (USA)
720) Pochette en couleur d'un enregistrement de blues. (USA)
721) Pochette d'un disque de chansons par une formation beat. (FRA)
722) Pochette pour l'enregistrement d'un culte célébré la veille du Sabbat. (USA)
723) Pochette d'un disque sur Chicago. Teintes métalliques. (USA)
724) Pochette pour un enregistrement de chansons par un chanteur noir. (USA)
725) Pochette d'un disque de deux chanteurs populaires. (USA)

**Record Covers
Schallplattenhüllen
Pochettes de disques**

726

727

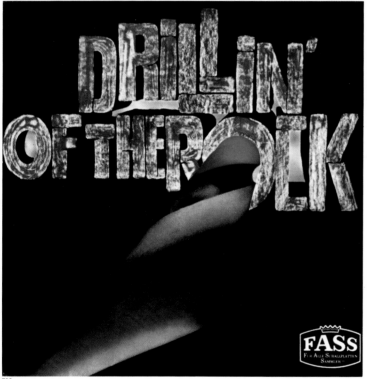

728

729

Artist / Künstler / Artiste:

726) KIM WHITESIDES/ACY LEHMAN
727) PETER SCHAUMANN/ROBERT L. HEIMALL
728) KLAUS WITT
729) TOM WILSON/NICK FASCIANO
730) 731) WALTER GRIEDER
732) 736) HEINZ HUKE
733) 734) 737) HEINZ STIEGER
735) IGNAZIO GOMEZ/JOHN LEPREVOST

Art Director / Directeur artistique:

726) ACY LEHMAN
727) WILLIAM S. HARVEY
728) WILFRIED MANNES
729) JOHN BERG
730) 731) WALTER GRIEDER
733) 734) 737) OSWALD DUBACHER
735) JOHN LEPREVOST

Agency / Agentur / Agence – Studio:

732) 736) TOSTMANN WERBEAGENTUR GMBH, HANNOVER/GER
735) UNIVERSAL STUDIOS, LOS ANGELES

Publisher / Verleger / Editeur:

726) RCA RECORDS, NEW YORK
727) NONESUCH RECORDS, NEW YORK
728) PHONOGRAM TONGESELLSCHAFT MBH, HAMBURG
729) COLUMBIA RECORDS, NEW YORK
730) 731) TELL RECORD, BASEL
732) 736) DEUTSCHE GRAMMOPHON GMBH, HAMBURG
733) 734) 737) EX LIBRIS VERLAG AG, ZÜRICH
735) KAPP RECORDS, UNIVERSAL CITY, CALIF.

726) Record cover for music by a popular group. (USA)
727) Record cover for concertos composed around the psalms of David. Full colour. (USA)
728) Cover for a recording of popular music. (GER)
729) Cover for recordings by a famous local blues singer. Full colour. (USA)
730) 731) Record covers for fairy tales retold in a Swiss dialect. Full colour. (SWI)
732) Record cover in pop colours for a selection of pop hits from 1970. (GER)
733) 734) Record covers in bright colours from a series of puppet-show tales for children. (SWI)
735) Complete record cover in pop Arcimboldo style for renderings by a beat group. (USA)
736) Record cover for songs by two old favourites. Yellow, red and white on black. (GER)
737) Record cover for children's bedtime stories. Bright colours. (SWI)

730

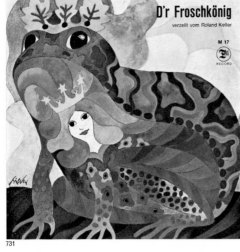

731

732

733

734

735

736

737

726) Hülle für Musikstücke einer populären Gruppe. (USA)
727) Mehrfarbige Hülle für zu den Psalmen Davids komponierte Konzerte. (USA)
728) Hülle für eine Aufnahme populärer Musik. (GER)
729) Schallplattenumschlag für einen berühmten Sänger von Blues. Mehrfarbig. (USA)
730) 731) Schallplattenhüllen für im Schweizer Dialekt erzählte Märchen. Mehrfarbige Illustrationen. (SWI)
732) Schallplattenumschlag in Pop-Farben für eine Sammlung von Pop-Schlagern des Jahres 1970. (GER)
733) 734) In fröhlichen Farben gehaltene Plattenhüllen für eine Serie von Kasperlitheater-Stücken. (SWI)
735) Vollständige, bunte Hülle im Pop-Stil für Darbietungen einer Beat-Gruppe. (USA)
736) Hülle für Schlager, dargeboten von zwei altbekannten Favoriten. Gelb, rot, weiss auf Schwarz. (GER)
737) Schallplattenumschlag in lebhaften, bunten Farben für Gutenacht-Geschichten. (SWI)

726) Pochette d'un disque d'airs à la mode. (USA)
727) Pochette pour deux concertos composés d'après les psaumes de David. Polychrome. (USA)
728) Pochette d'un disque de musique populaire. (GER)
729) Pochette pour un enregistrement d'un chanteur de blues. Polychrome. (USA)
730) 731) Pochettes pour des contes racontés en dialecte suisse-allemand. Polychrome. (SWI)
732) Pochette pour une sélection de «hits» de 1970. Couleurs pop. (GER)
733) 734) Pochettes de couleurs vives pour un théâtre de marionnettes. (SWI)
735) Vue complète d'une pochette pour un disque de musique pop. (USA)
736) Pochette d'un disque de deux chanteurs populaires. Jaune, rouge et blanc sur noir. (GER)
737) Pochette d'un disque d'histoires à raconter le soir aux enfants. Couleurs vives. (SWI)

5

Trade Marks and Symbols

Letterheads

Packaging

Calendars

Christmas Cards

Schutzmarken

Briefköpfe

Packungen

Kalender

Glückwunschkarten

Marques et emblèmes

En-têtes

Emballages

Calendriers

Cartes de vœux

738) Logotype for Fredda Weiss, styling for print and television. (USA)
739) Trade mark for Faxon, Inc., Dallas. (USA)
740) Trade mark for Eskil Ohlsson Assoc. (USA)
741) Trade mark for Hortors Ltd., a South African conglomerate in the field of communications. (SAF)
742) Trade mark for Marineland Aquarium Products, Hollywood. (USA)
743) Trade mark for *Technolin* technical ropes and cables. (POL)
744) Trade mark for Keeble Cable Television Ltd. (USA)
745) Trade mark for York Gymnastic Club, Toronto. (CAN)
746) Trade mark for Summit Films, a company specializing in documentary skiing and mountaineering films. (USA)
747) Trade mark for a division of Smith, Kline & French, makers of pharmaceuticals. (USA)
748) Logotype for DIAMOND IDEAS, newsletter issued by De Beers Consolidated Mines Ltd. (USA)
749) Trade mark for Sound Investment, a company specializing in stereo tape equipment. (GB)
750) Logotype for Fratelli Faver, Lucca, a ceramic tile manufacturer. (ITA)
751) Logotype for a house organ published by American Broadcasting Co. (USA)

738) Signet für Fredda Weiss, Beratung in Stilfragen für Druck und Fernsehen. (USA)
739) Schutzmarke der Firma Faxon, Inc., Dallas. (USA)
740) Schutzmarke für die Firma Eskil Ohlsson Assoc. (USA)
741) Schutzmarke für eine südafrikanische Firma, die als Beratungsstelle für Fragen der Kommunikation tätig ist. (SAF)
742) Schutzmarke eines Unternehmens, das Produkte für Aquarien liefert. (USA)
743) Schutzmarke für *Technolin*, technische Seile und Kabel. (POL)
744) Schutzmarke für die Keeble Cable Television Ltd. (USA)
745) Schutzmarke eines kanadischen Gymnastik-Clubs. (CAN)
746) Schutzmarke für einen Filmproduzenten, der sich auf Dokumentarfilme über den Ski- und Berg-Sport spezialisiert. (USA)
747) Schutzmarke für eine Abteilung eines Produzenten von Pharmazeutika. (USA)
748) Siegel für DIAMOND IDEAS, Informationsbulletin der De Beers Consolidated Mines Ltd. (USA)
749) Schutzmarke eines Lieferanten von Geräten für Stereobänder. (GB)
750) Siegel der Firma Fratelli Faver, Lucca, Produzent von Keramikplatten. (ITA)
751) Siegel für die Hauszeitschrift einer amerikanischen Radiogesellschaft. (USA)

738) Logotype de Fredda Weiss, styliste pour l'imprimerie et la télévision. (USA)
739) Marque de la société Faxon, Inc., Dallas. (USA)
740) Marque de la société Eskil Ohlsson Assoc. (USA)
741) Marque d'une société-conseil en matière de communications. (SAF)
742) Emblème d'un fournisseur d'articles pour les aquariums. (USA)
743) Marque de *Technolin*, câbles et cordages techniques. (POL)
744) Marque de la Keeble Cable Television Ltd. (USA)
745) Emblème d'un club de gymnastique. (CAN)
746) Marque d'une société de production cinématographique, spécialisée dans les films sur le ski et l'alpinisme. (USA)
747) Emblème d'une des divisions d'un laboratoire pharmaceutique. (USA)
748) Logotype pour DIAMOND IDEAS, bulletin de la De Beers Consolidated Mines Ltd. (USA)
749) Marque d'un fournisseur d'équipement stéréophonique. (GB)
750) Logotype de la société Fratelli Faver, Lucca, fabricants de carreaux en céramique. (ITA)
751) Sigle pour le journal d'entreprise d'un émetteur radiophonique. (USA)

739

740

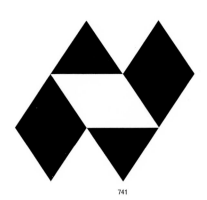

741

742

738

751

743

747

744

748

745

749

746

750

Artist | Künstler | Artiste:

738) THOMAS CARNASE/IRWIN GOLDBERG
739) CRAWFORD DUNN
740) ESKIL OHLSSON
741) 746) JOHN R. RIEBEN
742) ADRIAN LOOS DESIGN STUDIO
743) WLADYSLAW STAŇCZYKOWSKI
744) GLEN ARNOLD
745) RICHARD JANIS
747) 748) ROGER COOK/DON SHANOSKY
749) MICHAEL PACEY
750) MICHELE PROVINCIALI
751) GEORGE MCGINNIS

Art Director | Directeur artistique:

739) CRAWFORD DUNN
741) 746) JOHN R. RIEBEN
742) ADRIAN LOOS DESIGN STUDIO
744) E. J. MORRISON
745) RICHARD JANIS
747) ALAN KLAWANS
749) JEFF YOUNG
750) MINALE, TATTERSFIELD, PROVINCIALI LTD.
751) GEORGE MCGINNIS

Agency | Agentur | Agence – Studio:

738) NADLER & LARIMER, INC., NEW YORK
739) CRAWFORD DUNN ASSOC., DALLAS
741) 746) UNIMARK INTERNATIONAL, DENVER
742) J. BYK ADV., LOS ANGELES
744) STEWART & MORRISON LTD., TORONTO
745) RICHARD JANIS STUDIO, TORONTO
747) 748) COOK & SHANOSKY ASSOC., INC., NEW YORK
749) ASTRA ARTS, LOS ANGELES
750) MINALE, TATTERSFIELD, PROVINCIALI LTD., LONDON

Advertiser | Auftraggeber | Client:

738) FREDDA WEISS, NEW YORK
739) FAXON, INC., DALLAS
740) ESKIL OHLSSON ASSOC., INC., NEW YORK
741) HORTORS LTD., JOHANNESBURG/SAF
742) MARINELAND AQUARIUM PRODUCTS,
     HOLLYWOOD, CALIF.
743) TECHNOLIN, LÓDZ
744) KEEBLE CABLE TELEVISION LTD., TORONTO
745) YORK GYMNASTIC CLUB, TORONTO
746) SUMMIT FILMS, DENVER
747) SMITH, KLINE & FRENCH LABORATOIRES,
     PHILADELPHIA
748) DE BEERS CONSOLIDATED MINES LTD., NEW YORK
749) SOUND INVESTMENT, VAN NUYS, CALIF.
750) FRATELLI FAVRE, LUCCA/ITA
751) AMERICAN BROADCASTING CO., NEW YORK

Trade Marks and Symbols
Schutzmarken und Signete
Marques et emblèmes

752

Artist | Künstler | Artiste:

752) JIM DONOAHUE
753) RICHARD WICKSTROM
754) MARGARET MALAST/
      ALAN PECKOLICK
755) TOMAS VELLVE
756) KAZUMASA NAGAI
757) 759) JOHN R. RIEBEN
758) CLAUDE DIETRICH
760) MANFRED GOTTHAUS
761) IAN VALENTINE
762) ARNOLD SAKS, INC./
      TOMAS NITTNER
763) JEAN FORTIN
764) CAREY COREA
765) BOBBIE HAZELTINE/
      ROD LAMBETH
766) CLAUDE-HENRI SAUNIER
767) HARRY ZELENKO

752) Trade mark for a typographer, Typographic Quebec Ltd. (CAN)
753) Trade mark for a division of Singer-Link. (USA)
754) Logotype for Time Equities, Inc. (USA)
755) Logotype for Moro Asociad Cataluña. (SPA)
756) Trade mark for a maker of skis, Kaneda Ski Seisakujo. (JAP)
757) Trade mark for Huletts Ltd., sugar manufacturers. (SAF)
758) Trade mark for Prolansa, Lima, makers of wire products. (PER)
759) Trade mark for a land development project near Cochiti City. (USA)
760) Trade mark for the Cooper Construction Company. (CAN)
761) Trade mark for the Meridian Building Group Ltd. (CAN)
762) Logotype for Benjamin and Zicherman, consulting engineers. (USA)
763) Trade mark for the *Rhône-Poulenc* group (see also figs. 432 and 433). (FRA)
764) Mark for Domine Builders Supply Corp., makers of concrete blocks. (USA)
765) Trade mark for the Allen Center, Houston. (USA)
766) Trade mark for the *Gaster* supermarket in Nancy. (FRA)
767) Symbol for the André Emmerich Gallery, Inc. (USA)

752) Schutzmarke für einen Typographen. (CAN)
753) Schutzmarke für eine Abteilung der Singer-Link. (USA)
754) Siegel für die Firma Time Equities, Inc. (USA)
755) Siegel für die Firma Moro Asociad Cataluña. (SPA)
756) Schutzmarke für einen Hersteller von Skis. (JAP)
757) Schutzmarke für einen Zucker-Produzenten. (SAF)
758) Schutzmarke für einen Hersteller von Draht-Produkten. (PER)
759) Siegel für Überbauungs-Projekte (nach altmexikanischen Motiven). (USA)
760) Schutzmarke einer Baugesellschaft. (CAN)
761) Schutzmarke einer Vereinigung von Firmen der Baubranche. (CAN)
762) Siegel einer Firma für technische Beratung. (USA)
763) Schutzmarke für *Rhône-Poulenc* (siehe auch Abb. 432 und 433). (FRA)
764) Schutzmarke für die Firma Domine Builders Supply Corp. (USA)
765) Schutzmarke für das Allen Center, Houston. (USA)
766) Schutzmarke des Supermarktes *Gaster*, Nancy. (FRA)
767) Signet für die Galerie André Emmerich. (USA)

752) Emblème d'un atelier de typographie. (CAN)
753) Marque de la société Singer-Link. (USA)
754) Sigle de la société Times Equities, Inc. (USA)
755) Logotype pour Moro Asociad Cataluña. (SPA)
756) Marque d'un fabricant de skis. (JAP)
757) Marque de fabrique d'une sucrerie. (SAF)
758) Emblème d'un fabricant de produits en fil de fer. (PER)
759) Sigle pour un projet de développement urbain. (USA)
760) Emblème d'une entreprise de construction. (CAN)
761) Emblème d'une association d'entreprises du bâtiment. (CAN)
762) Sigle de Benjamin and Zicherman, ingénieurs-conseils. (USA)
763) Emblème de *Rhône-Poulenc* (voir ill. 432 et 433). (FRA)
764) Marque de la société Domine Builders Supply Corp. (USA)
765) Emblème du Allen Center, Houston. (USA)
766) Marque du supermarché *Gaster* à Nancy. (FRA)
767) Sigle de la galerie André Emmerich. (USA)

Trade Marks and Symbols
Schutzmarken und Signete
Marques et emblèmes

753

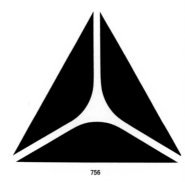

756

754

757

755

758

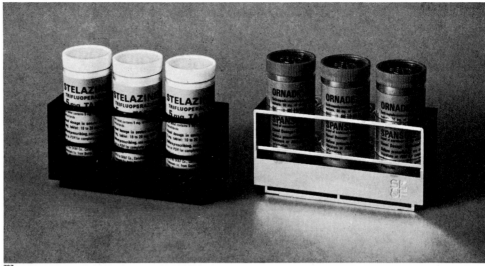

795

797

798

796

799

Art Director | Directeur artistique:

791) BILL SWENEY
792) FRITZ GOTTSCHALK
793) HANS KLEEFELD
794) EUROGRAPHIC LTD.
795) ORN VIDARSSON
796) JOHN DI GIANNI
797) WARREN BLAIR
798) JUNE FRASER
799) THOMAS F. COLEMAN

Agency | Agentur | Agence – Studio:

791) LAWLER BALLARD LITTLE ADVERTISING,
      ATLANTA, GA.
792) GOTTSCHALK + ASH LTD., MONTREAL
793) STEWART & MORRISON LTD., TORONTO
794) EUROGRAPHIC LTD., ROSS HULL/GB
795) PLAN DESIGN A/S, COPENHAGEN
796) GIANNINOTO ASSOC., NEW YORK
798) DESIGN RESEARCH UNIT, LONDON
799) IBM ROCHESTER DESIGN CENTER, ROCHESTER, N.Y.

**Packaging
Packungen
Emballages**

800

801

802

803

804

Artist | Künstler | Artiste:

800) JACQUES LECLERC
801) DAVID BROMIGE/GRAHAM SOUTHWORTH
802) 803) MONICA GRIMBURG-FLOOD/
      HOUSE OF HARLEY ART DEPT.
804) BUNSHICHI TOYOI/HIROZO SAIDA
805) FELIX BURKARD/NIKLAUS SCHMID

Art Director | Directeur artistique:

800) ROMAN CIESLEWICZ
801) DAVID BROMIGE/GRAHAM SOUTHWORTH
802) 803) GERALD ROSENFELD
804) HARUYO TAHIRA
805) FELIX BURKARD

Agency | Agentur | Agence – Studio:

800) MAFIA (MAIMÉ ARNODIN, FAYOLLE, INT.,
      ASSOC.), PARIS
801) GRAHAM SOUTHWORTH, DAVID BROMIGE &
      ASSOC., HITCHIN, HERTS./GB

Packaging
Packungen
Emballages

805

806

808

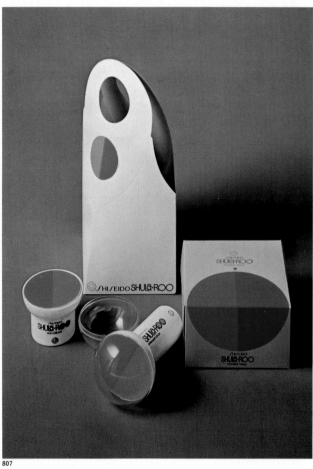

807

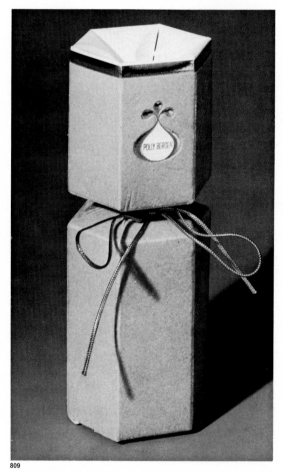

809

Artist | Künstler | Artiste :

806) MASAKAZU YAMASHITA
807) SHUNSAKU SUGIURA/KUNIO HACHIMURA/SHUICHI IKEDA
808) SILVIO COPPOLA
809) TOM ROBBINS/JIM THOMAS
810) 811) GEORGES LEMOINE

Art Director | Directeur artistique :

806) YASUI KUMAI
807) SHIGEYOSHI AOKI
808) SILVIO COPPOLA
809) TOM ROBBINS
810) 811) JACQUES LAVAUX

Agency | Agentur | Agence — Studio :

808) STUDIO COPPOLA, MILAN

Packaging / Packungen / Emballages

810

806) Set-up gift boxes for *Shiseido* cosmetics. (JAP)
807) Tube, jar, carton and bag for a range of *Shiseido* cosmetics for teenagers. (JAP)
808) Folding box for beach fashions. (ITA)
809) Two-in-one gift package for Polly Bergen, Los Angeles. (USA)
810) 811) Cover design and folding box for chocolates sold by a French department store. (FRA)

806) Verkaufsbereit aufgemachte Geschenkschachteln für *Shiseido*-Kosmetika. (JAP)
807) Tube, Dose, Packung und Tragtasche für *Shiseido*-Kosmetika für Teenagers. (JAP)
808) Faltschachtel als Tragtasche für Artikel der Bade-Mode. (ITA)
809) Zwillings-Geschenkpackung, von einer Firma der Verpackungsindustrie entwickelt. (USA)
810) 811) Bild und Schachtel einer Schokoladen-Weihnachtspackung für Kinder. (FRA)

806) Boîtes cadeaux à couvercles cloches pour des produits cosmétiques *Shiseido*. (JAP)
807) Tube, pot, carton et cabas pour des produits de beauté destinés aux jeunes. (JAP)
808) Boîte pliante pour des vêtements de plage de la maison Telerie Zucchi, Milan. (ITA)
809) Emballage cadeau double, conçu par une entreprise de conditionnement. (USA)
810) 811) Illustration et boîte pliante pour les chocolats vendus à Noël dans les magasins *Prisunic*. (FRA)

811

812

813

812) Folding boxes for *Roche* psychotropic drugs. (SWI)
813) Carton for bottles of port wine. (GER)
814) Slipcase for a standard colour atlas and supplement. (GER)
815) Bottle styling and folding boxes for two versions of a hair lotion. (GER)
816) Bottle and label for a new, specially brewed beer. (SWI)
817) Retail package for *Leggs* panty hose, with a play on the word '(L)eggs'. (USA)
818)–820) Labels for a white wine, a local wine and a Swiss burgundy. (SWI)
821) Carton for a bottle of white wine from the Paul Masson Vineyards. (USA)
822) Label for a jar of plums in armagnac. Purple plum, yellow ground, red and tawny lettering, green and blue ornament. (FRA)

812) Faltschachteln für *Roche*-Psychopharmaka. (SWI)
813) Mit blindgeprägter Goldfolie kaschierte Verkaufspackung für Portoweine der Firma Henkell & Co., Wiesbaden. (GER)
814) Einsteckschachtel für einen farbigen Atlas und Nachträge der Farbwerke Hoechst AG. (GER)
815) Flasche und Packung für zwei Sorten Haarwasser der Firma Dr. G. Dralle, Hamburg. (GER)
816) Flasche und Etikett für ein Spezialbräu der Bier-Interessengemeinschaft Lubi AG, Zürich. (SWI)
817) Verkaufspackung für eine Strumpfhose. (USA)
818)–820) Weinetiketts der Druckerei Roth & Sautter, Lausanne. (SWI)
821) Packung für eine Flasche Weisswein der Keltereien Paul Masson. (USA)
822) Etikett für einen Topf mit in Armagnac eingelegten Pflaumen. (FRA)

812) Boites pliantes pour des psychotropes *Roche*. (SWI)
813) Carton laminé d'une feuille d'or gaufrée à sec, pour du porto. (GER)
814) Etui pour un atlas en couleur et ses suppléments. (GER)
815) Habillages de flacons et boîtes pliantes pour deux types de lotion capillaire. (GER)
816) Bouteille et étiquette pour une nouvelle bière spéciale. (SWI)
817) Emballage de vente pour des collants. (USA)
818)–820) Etiquettes pour du vin. (SWI)
821) Carton pour une bouteille de vin blanc américain. (USA)
822) Etiquette pour un bocal de prunes à l'armagnac. Prune mauve, fond jaune, texte en rouge et bronze, décoration en vert et bleu. (FRA)

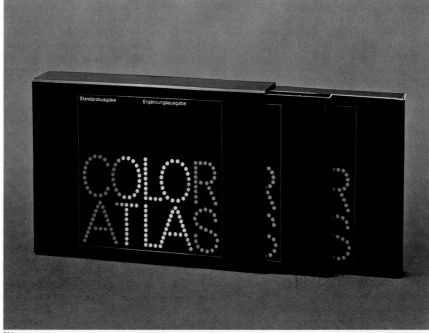

814

Artist | Künstler | Artiste:

812) SYLVIA GOESCHKE
813) ATELIER SCHEIBE
814) HANS-PETER WEIBLEN
815) E + U HIESTAND
816) F. STEINER
817) ROGER FERRITER
818) ERNEST WITZIG
819) ROBERT HÉRITIER/BENI SCHALCHER
820) ROBERT HÉRITIER/EMANUEL BOSSHART
821) DANNY BHANG/JEROME GOULD

815

816

817

Sélectionné à la production

818

819

820

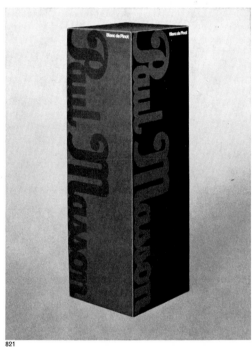

821

822

Art Director / Directeur artistique:

812) JACQUES HAUSER
813) RICHARD SCHEIBE
814) HANS-PETER WEIBLEN
815) E + U HIESTAND
816) MAX RINDLISBACHER
817) ROGER FERRITER
818) 819) MICHEL LOGOZ
820) MAX ROTH
821) JEROME GOULD

Agency / Agentur / Agence – Studio:

812) HUMBERT & VOGT, RIEHEN/SWI
815) E + U HIESTAND, ZÜRICH
816) GISLER & GISLER, ZÜRICH
817) LUBALIN, SMITH, CARNASE & FERRITER, NEW YORK
818)–820) ROTH + SAUTER S.A., LAUSANNE
821) GOULD, JEROME, & ASSOC., INC., LOS ANGELES
822) JEANBIN IMPRIMERIE, PARIS

223

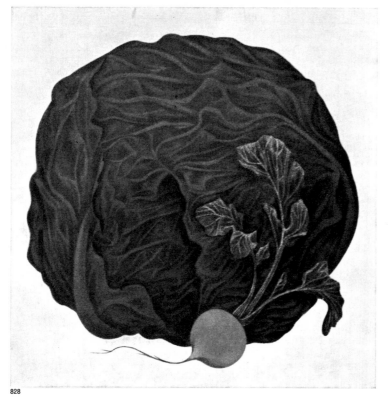

Art Director | Directeur artistique:

823)–825) R. J. DAVIDSON
826) 829) BERNARD VANGRIN
827) 828) TADASHI OHASHI
830) HIROSHI OHCHI
831) SHIGERU AKIZUKI
832) ILIO NEGRI

Agency | Agentur | Agence – Studio:

826) 829) KETCHUM, MACLEOD & GROVE, INC., PITTSBURGH, PA
827) 828) AKIZUKI DESIGN OFFICE, TOKYO
832) STUDIO NEGRI, MILAN

830

Calendar '71

831

Calendars / Kalender
Calendriers

Artist | Künstler | Artiste:

823)–825) R. J. DAVIDSON
826) 829) ARNOLD VARGA
827) 828) TADASHI OHASHI
830) HIROSHI OHCHI
831) SHIGERU AKIZUKI
832) ILIO NEGRI

823)–825) Complete sheet and two illustrations (full colour) for a small calendar for Halvin Co., New York, importers of wines and spirits. (USA)
826) 829) Sheets from a calendar for the Scott Paper Company presenting Americana, here winter memories and ghosts. Full colour. (USA)
827) 828) Sheet and illustration from a calendar for Kikkoman Shoyu Co., makers of soy sauce. (JAP)
830) Sheet of a calendar designed by the artist as a gift to friends. Fluorescent colours. (JAP)
831) Wall calendar in muted colours for the Daiichi Sogo Bank. (JAP)
832) One side of a calendar with phases of the moon for *Syntex* pharmaceuticals. (ITA)

823)–825) Blatt und mehrfarbige Illustration aus einem Kalender für einen Wein- und Spirituosen-Importeur. (USA)
826) 829) Mehrfarbige Blätter aus dem Kalender einer Papierfabrik. Motto: Amerikana, hier Winter-Erinnerungen und Gespenster. (USA)
827) 828) Blatt und Illustration (violett) aus dem Kalender eines Saucenfabrikanten. (JAP)
830) Blatt in Leuchtfarben aus einem Kalender, den der Künstler an Freunde verschenkte. (JAP)
831) Wandkalender einer Bank. (JAP)
832) Seite eines langformatigen Kalenders mit entsprechenden Mondphasen für *Syntex*-Pharmazeutika. Mehrfarbig auf blauem Grund. (ITA)

823)–825) Page et deux illustrations polychromes du calendrier d'un importeur new-yorkais de vins et spiritueux. (USA)
826) 829) Pages du calendrier d'une fabrique de papier, présentant des «américana», ici des souvenirs d'hiver et des fantômes. (USA)
827) 828) Page et illustration du calendrier d'un fabricant de sauces au soja. (JAP)
830) Page d'un calendrier créé par l'artiste à l'intention de ses amis. (JAP)
831) Calendrier mural pour une banque. (JAP)
832) Page d'un calendrier indiquant les phases de la lune, pour les produits pharmaceutiques *Syntex*. Polychrome sur fond bleu. (ITA)

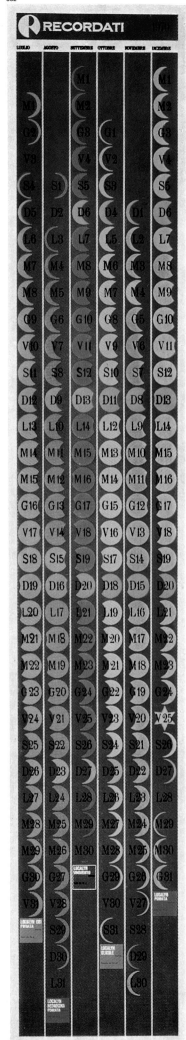

832

833

835

834

836

833)–836) Sheet and three illustrations from a calendar showing landscapes by Darigo in the manner of famous artists. (FRA)
837) Calendar for Expo 67 in Montreal, shown flat and assembled. (CAN)
838) Wall calendar with full-colour illustration alluding to Swiss folk customs. (SWI)
839) 840) Desk calendar for CBS, shown closed and open. The cover is laminated with aluminium foil. (USA)
841) 842) Two sheets from a *Mobil* calendar showing 'patent and comical things'. Illustrations in full colour, blue and red dates. (AUS)

833)–836) Vollständiges Blatt und drei Illustrationen aus einem Kalender mit von Darigo im Stil berühmter Maler konzipierten Bildern, hier von berühmten Plätzen in Paris. (FRA)
837) Kalender (flach und zusammengesetzt) für die Expo 67 in Montreal. (CAN)
838) Wandkalender der Offsetdruckerei H. Weiss-Stauffacher, Basel, mit mehrfarbiger Illustration als Hinweis auf schweizerische Volksbräuche. (SWI)
839) 840) Pultkalender (geschlossen und offen) der Columbia Broadcasting System, CBS. Der Umschlag ist mit einer Aluminiumfolie kaschiert und mit eingeritztem Schriftzeichen und Signet versehenen. (USA)
841) 842) Zwei Blätter aus einem humoristischen Kalender der Mobil Oil über «patente und komische Dinge». Mehrfarbige Illustrationen mit roten und blauen Daten. (AUS)

833)–836) Page et trois illustrations d'un calendrier pour Jean Lavigne, Paris. Illustrations de Darigo, à la manière d'artistes célèbres. (FRA)
837) Calendrier pour l'Expo 67 de Montréal, vu déplié et assemblé. (CAN)
838) Calendrier mural d'une imprimerie, illustrant en couleur le folklore suisse. (SWI)
839) 840) Agenda de bureau de la CBS, vu ouvert et fermé. Couverture laminée d'une feuille d'aluminium, gravée au sigle de la compagnie. (USA)
841) 842) Deux pages d'un calendrier humoristique pour la Mobil Oil, présentant «des choses comiques et ingénieuses». Illustrations polychromes, dates en bleu et rouge. (AUS)

837

6

TV and Film Advertising

Fernseh- und Filmwerbung

TV et films publicitaires

868-870

Artist | Künstler | Artiste:

862)–867) GRAHAM CLARKE
868)–870) ETIENNE DELESSERT
871)–876) RICHARD BAILEY
877)–880) GEORGE WALLDER
881)–884) GEOFF DUNBAR

Art Director | Directeur artistique:

862)–867) CLARKE/CLEMENTS/HUGHES
868)–870) IVAN HORVATH
877)–880) GEORGE WALLDER
881)–884) JOHN HALAS

Agency | Agentur | Agence – Studio:

862)–367) PETER MASSON & PARTNERS, LONDON
868)–870) OGILVY & MATHER, INC., NEW YORK
877)–880) A-T-V GRAPHIC DESIGN DEPT.,
          BOREHAMWOOD, HERTS/GB
881)–884) HALAS & BATCHELOR ANIMATION LTD., LONDON

Producer | Produktion | Production:

862)–867) CLARKE/CLEMENTS/HUGHES,
          MAIDSTONE, KENT/GB
868)–870) IVAN HORVATH/TOM BRENNAN/ELEKTRA FILM
          PRODUCTIONS, INC., NEW YORK
871)–876) PAUL WATSON/BBC T.V., LONDON
877)–880) A-T-V NETWORK LTD., BOREHAMWOOD, HERTS/GB
881)–884) HALAS & BATCHELOR ANIMATION LTD., LONDON

877-880

881-884

Film / Television / Fernsehen

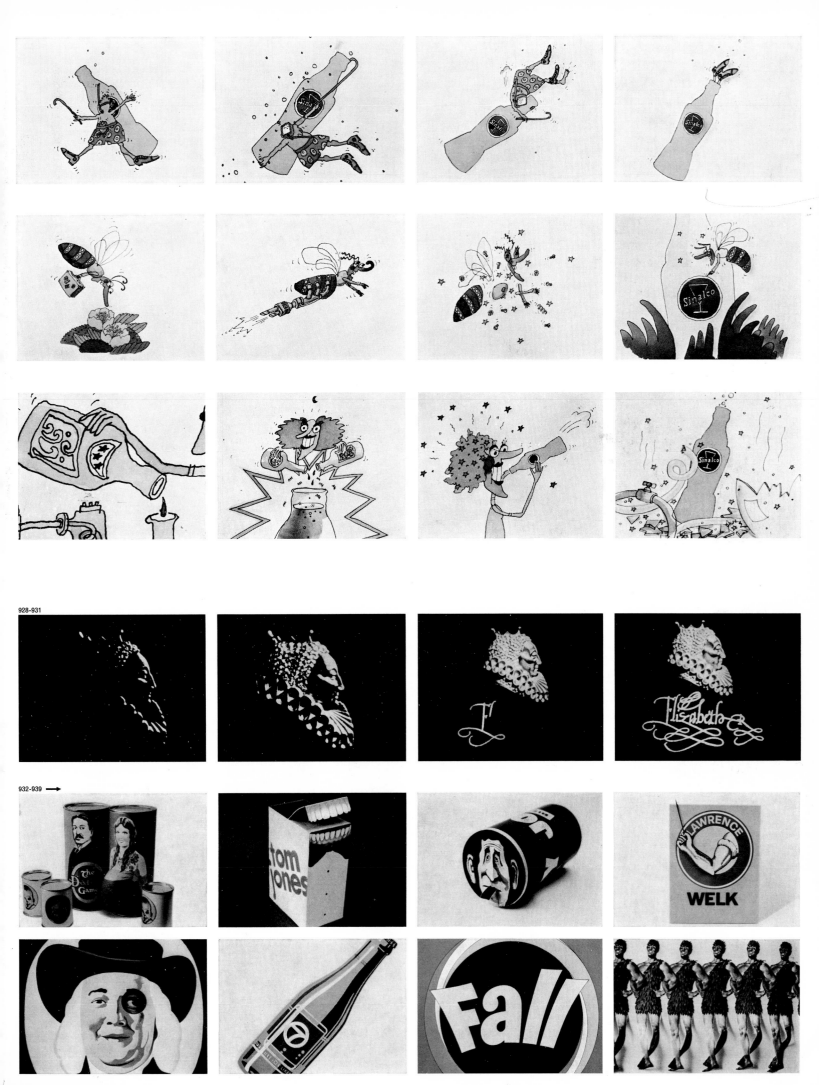

928-931

932-939 →